Discovery

A Daily Bible Study And Prayer Guide

CRUSADE EDITION

Published by
World Wide Publications
1313 Hennepin Avenue
Minneapolis, Minnesota 55403

A selection of Scripture
readings from the Old
and New Testaments,
with expository comment,
to guide you in the
adventure of daily
Bible reading and prayer

Copyright © 1974 by

Scripture Union U.S.A.
1716 Spruce Street
Philadelphia, Pennsylvania 19103

Library of Congress Catalogue Card Number

74-22998

Canadian address: Scripture Union
2100 Lawrence Ave. East
Scarborough, Ontario M1R 2Z7

Discovery *is your invitation to the adventure of daily Bible reading and prayer. Most Christians acknowledge that reading the Scriptures and talking with God regularly are indispensable for spiritual growth, but many lack practical help. SCRIPTURE UNION has been providing such help for 108 years, and today its ministry extends to 78 countries.*

By special arrangement with Scripture Union, the BILLY GRAHAM EVANGELISTIC ASSOCIATION joyfully makes this Souvenir Edition available to you. The book contains a plan of readings covering representative portions from both the Old and New Testaments, combined with a Christ-centered commentary for each passage. It is our prayer that **DISCOVERY** *will guide you into a deeper relationship to God, and into more complete obedience to his Son Jesus Christ.*

Your Daily Bible Readings

(in order of appearance)

*In this book are 183 Daily Scripture Readings —
enough to guide you through six months of daily
Bible reading and prayer.*

How To Use This Book

Bible reading and prayer is two-way communication. Through the Scriptures, God speaks to you; in prayer, you speak to God. This should not be simply a religious exercise; it is, rather, an essential means for strengthening your discipleship.

We suggest that you set aside a time each day for personal worship, preferably first thing in the morning. The following *Guide for Daily Worship* will help you structure your time alone with God:

Pray before reading, asking God to help you to understand and receive his Word. You may wish to use this adaptation of the Psalmist's ancient prayer (Psalm 119:18): "Father, open my eyes, that I may behold wondrous things out of thy Law," for Jesus Christ's sake. Amen.

Read carefully the day's Scripture passage. Refer to the preceding and following selections in order to understand fully the context of today's reading.

Meditate on what you have read, waiting in openness, ready to obey God's Word to you. *First,* think about the passage by asking yourself such questions as:

- What is the main point of this passage?

- What does God — Father, Son and Holy Spirit — reveal of himself?

- What insight am I given into myself, and into my life situation?

- What does Christ require of me here and now? Is there a command to obey or a promise to claim? Is there an error to avoid, an example to follow?

Next complete your meditation by reading the **Discovery** comment for the day. In light of these insights from your fellow Christians, think further about what God is saying to you. It will help you to record your findings in a notebook, listing your thoughts and noting any action you should take.

Pray again. This time, turn the things you have learned into prayers. Thank God for his greatness and his love. Confess your sins. Remember the needs of others. Adore the Lord in his beauty. Go forth to serve him with joy!

When you have finished the readings in this book, you will want to continue the practice of daily Bible reading and prayer.

Your Introduction to John

Who wrote it? John and his brother James were two of Jesus' disciples. What is interesting, though, is that they were wild men — wanting to tell other people what to do, willing to call down fire from heaven on people, and so on. Jesus even nicknamed them the "Sons of Thunder"! But after Jesus got to work on John, he was completely different. He became known as the "apostle of love," and the letters he wrote are full of love. So when he tells us in his Gospel what Jesus can do for people, he knows what he's talking about!

Why did he write it? He wrote this Gospel so that we could come to know Jesus as the Savior of the world, and so that we could find new life in him. He wants us to be changed, just as he himself has been changed. And — *more people come to faith in Jesus Christ through the Gospel according to John than through any other part of the Bible*. So, as you read it, expect God to speak to you, too.

Our Notes will cover the first six chapters of John, which introduce us to the unique origins of Jesus, the beginning of his ministry, and to some of the amazing things he did and the people he met. Be sure to read the rest of the Gospel in your spare time. It's worth it.

The Focal Point

John wastes no time before introducing us to the One his book is about. Jesus is in the first verse of this Gospel, and the last verse, and in most verses in between! Is Christ central in your life like that? Does everything revolve around him?

● **Who Christ is** (1-5). We begin with Christ way back in eternity, truly God, living in glory with his Father. From there we see him bringing this universe into being, giving men their life and every "light" they live by. John wants us to know he is not writing about "just a man," but about "God come in the flesh"!

● **How Christ came** (6-11). Not in a blaze of glory! No royal herald announced his arrival — just "a man named John"! Christ came, unrecognized and unwanted, even by his own chosen people. A failure, then? "No," says John, "read on!"

● **What Christ does** (12-13). These verses sum up what this Gospel is all about: *new life for all who become committed to Jesus Christ!* Perhaps you have heard someone say after a successful operation: "I feel like a new person!" After Christ's "heart-operation," you can say the same — only more so!

Prayer

I thank You, Father, for my creation, preservation, and all the blessings of this life; but above all for Your Son, my Lord Jesus Christ. Amen.

Keynote

And still the light shines

God's Son and God's Servant

In order to help you regularly use the questions in the *Guide* at the front of your Notes, let us use two of them now, and just change them slightly.

What do I learn about Christ?

He is full of truth. This doesn't just mean "he tells the truth." It means he is the only One who shows us all the truth about God. See verse 14. That is why he is called "the Word," as verse 18 explains.

He is full of grace. The point here is that Jesus doesn't just help us to understand about God; he actually helps us to *experience* God in a rich and personal way. That's what verse 16 is all about.

What do I learn about myself?

If Christ is all that, I must know him. You see, Christ came so that I might know God. But if that is to happen, he must come to me, and also I must come to him. I must receive or take all that he came to bring me (16).

If Christ is all that, I must make him known. One gets the impression that John the Baptist lived for just one thing — to make it possible for other people to know Jesus Christ. May God give me a strong reason for living, like John's.

Prayer

I thank You today, Lord Jesus, that You stooped so low as to become flesh and blood for my sake. Amen.

Keynote

To know Christ and make him known

What John Said about Jesus

Get hold of two things John says about Jesus, and you will have grasped the very heart of the Christian faith! Here they are:

● **"Behold, the Lamb of God, who takes away the sin of the world"** (29). If I want to get anywhere with God I must learn that I can never "pay" for my own sin. The pollution in my life is like an enormous mortgage that I can never pay off, no matter how long I live. But Jesus, like one of the lambs in the Old Testament sacrifices, carried away all the guilt and the shame of my sin when he died on the cross. Point One: because of Calvary I can have a clean slate!

● **"This is he who baptizes with the Holy Spirit"** (33). If Point One were all there was to it, we might find it rather depressing. We would keep trying to "go straight," we would fail most of the time, and we would need dozens of "clean slates" every day! But there is more. As my heart is opened to Christ, I am "baptized with the Holy Spirit." That means God's own Spirit comes into my life, to bring me the power I need for each day! Point Two: through Jesus Christ, life can really become "new"!

Prayer

I thank You, dear God, for all the blessings that came to the world by Jesus Christ. Amen.

Keynote

Pardon — and power

Finding and Following

● **See the disciples finding Jesus!** Read Andrew's words in verse 41, and Philip's in verse 45. What a discovery! Have *you* made it? Have you actually come to know him as a real Person, alive today and sharing your life with you? (The best way to look for him sometimes is on your knees.)

● **See Jesus finding the disciples!** Interesting, isn't it, that Philip thought he had found Jesus, when all the time Jesus had found him (43)! There's a deep truth there. Getting to know Christ is not so much a matter of trying to find him, as of letting him find us! (That, too, often happens when you are on your knees.)

● **See the disciples finding each other!** Read verses 41 and 45. In the first case, Andrew was so excited at finding Jesus that he went immediately to find his *close relative,* Simon. In the second case, Philip was so excited that he went and told his *close friend,* Nathanael. Please look around you. Is there someone close to you whom you haven't told about Jesus Christ?

After *finding* comes *following* (37,43). What does that mean? It means listening to him, doing what he says, and becoming more like him as you get to know him.

Prayer

Lord Jesus, make me a missionary for You among my friends and my family. For Your name's sake. Amen.

Keynote

"He brought him to Jesus"

Our Power Ends, Christ's Power Begins

● **Our power ends.** "The wine gave out" (3). Is that how it is? We've run dry. Anything we ever had to give to others has come to an end. People who look to us for a lead are disappointed. We can't go on like this; *something's* got to happen!

● **Christ's power begins.** It's only when our own strength runs out that we let Christ get to work (3). You put matters in his hands. Then you "do whatever he tells you" (5). That's where faith comes in. And as you go *he* does the miracle; the "new wine" is given, better than ever before. And you cry to him, "You have kept the best wine till now" (10)!

A project: *Find out what the Bible teaches about wine.* In itself, it is one of God's gifts (Psalm 104:14-15). Christ, in this his first miracle, made over 120 gallons of it! He drank with those he was out to reach, and was called a "winebibber" (or "drunkard") for doing so (Luke 7:33-34). But there are serious warnings about strong drink in Proverbs 20:1, Romans 14:21, Ephesians 5:18, and many other verses.

Prayer

Lord, how I need the sense of Your power in my life. Help me to understand how it is Your action in my life which is really best, for Your glory's sake. Amen.

Keynote

The obedience is ours; the miracle is his

Temples Must Be Clean

It's quite a shock to think that Christ's first miracle was supplying wine for a party; we think he is much too *serious* for things like that! Now comes another shock. Can you really picture Christ whipping those businessmen out of the Temple, throwing their money all over the floor, tipping over their tables? Many people think of him as much too *gentle* for that! But Christ was more balanced than we give him credit for; more balanced than we are, sometimes. He didn't attack trivial things like social fun; he went to the heart of things.

● **What Christ found.** He went right in and saw exactly what was going on (14). Religion in the Temple had become rotten at the core. But think for a moment of *yourself* as a kind of temple for God to live in (see 1 Corinthians 3:16-17). When Christ looks, what does he find deep inside (25)? How do you think he feels about it?

● **What Christ did.** Only one thing to be done — clear it all out! And so he did (15-16). Is a *whip* needed in your heart — things to be tipped over and cleaned out? Christ can do it; but you must let him in!

Prayer

Lord Jesus, there's so much to be put right. Give me the courage to tackle myself first, and then the world around me. Amen.

Keynote

Time for some house-cleaning?

New Life for All

What an exciting chapter this is! As we come to understand it, we'll catch the thrill of it.

● **The one thing that counts.** Here's one of the greatest truths Jesus taught. It is that belonging to God's Kingdom does not mean just

— trying to live a good life;

— going to church and praying;

— helping your neighbor.

But it is being *reborn* (3), having a brand-new life born within your heart, a brand-new orientation and focal point — Jesus Christ.

● **The two things that this means.** Read verse 5 again. Do you wonder what "born of water and the Spirit" means? It's not hard to understand:

The *water* means that your heart is washed or made clean.

The *Spirit* means that God puts his own Spirit in you to give you a dynamic new life.

The same two points were made in the Note on John 1:33.

Christ said, "You must be *born anew*" (7). Have you? ☐ Yes. ☐ No. ☐ Don't know. If No, or Don't know, *do something about it!* Verses 14 and 15 may help.

Prayer

Lord Jesus, You died that I might live. I put my trust in You now, for this very day and forever. Amen.

Keynote

No other door to the Kingdom

17

Hope for the Hopeless

VERSE OF THE WEEK
John 4:42

● **Here is despair!** How terrible verse 19 is, if it's really true. It does away with any idea that people are essentially good, or that people have only to see the good to love it. It looks as if the typical man is one who

loves his own will rather than God's;

prefers what he knows is wrong to what he knows is right;

chooses to get what he can out of this life, rather than considering the life to come.

Now look at what he is (18). "Condemned already!" That sounds pretty final.

● **Here is hope!** Verse 16 is where *God* steps in! Three things change the picture:

God's love — He loves the world as it is; he loves me *as I am.*

Christ's death — He did the impossible; he cleared my darkness away.

My faith — I believe in him and I trust in him.

On which side of the fence do you stand? If you are on *Christ's* side, verse 21 tells you what to do now. Yes, every deed must be "wrought in God" — that is, done in his strength and for his Kingdom.

Prayer

Lord, I want to belong to the new world, not the old. Help me to live in the light, and not in the darkness. Through Christ my Lord. Amen.

Keynote

Choose light, choose life!

How to Be Really Great

John the Baptist is one of the great men of the Bible. You can't help being impressed by him in today's passage. If you want to be great *in God's eyes,* as he was, you should —

● **Copy John's overriding ambition.** I think he had one desire: to get the job done that God had given him to do. Put together part of verse 28 and part of verse 26 to find what it was to *go before* Jesus and *bear witness* to him. He was not jealous of anyone else, even when his friends tried to make him feel bad (26). He didn't mind being "passed over for promotion"! Why not? And when his work was done, he was content to fade out. What a man!

● **Choose John's over-all motto.** His motto summed up his whole life; it's in verse 30. With a motto like this, you can't go wrong. Paul's motto was similar (Philippians 1:20).

● **Claim John's overflowing joy.** Think of it. John stands there and sees his followers drifting away one by one, going after Jesus, and he says, "My happiness is now complete" (29, *Phillips)!* You will find no greater joy in life than helping others to find Christ.

Prayer

Father, may my ambition in life be always to promote Christ, not myself. For his sake. Amen.

Keynote

A human signpost

Christ's Remedy for an Unsatisfying Existence

Many of us, like the woman in today's story, lead a life without much satisfaction. Perhaps, like her, we are —

● **Bound to tradition** (9) — tied to a way of life we didn't invent and never asked for, so we feel tied hand and foot;

● **Bound to the earth** (11) — so taken up with the business of *physical* survival and material gain that we can't hear when Christ talks of *heavenly* things;

● **Bound to routine** (15) — longing to get away from the daily grind. How did Christ help that woman? He didn't say, "Smash your water-pot against the wall and join a circus!" or tell her to break out and go wild, or join a protest movement, or head for a hippie haven in downtown Jerusalem!

If society's all wrong, you must change it from within, not by breaking *out* of it. And you must change *yourself* first — from within! Verse 14 is the key; it could be the answer for you.

What does he mean by "a spring of water"? Does John 7:37-39 help? He doesn't want to take the woman away from her water-pot, or her daily duties. He wants to give her his Spirit, his inner happiness, his abounding strength — *himself.*

Prayer

Lord Jesus, give me a better attitude to face the routines in my life. May they be transformed by the touch of Your hand. Amen.

Keynote

He takes the drudge out of drudgery

Facing Facts

You'll never get your life sorted out by burying your head in the sand. There was no shortcut for that woman to get the "living water" she needed; nor is there for you.

● **Take a good look at yourself.** Jesus *forced* the woman to, by his command in verse 16. He made her expose her sinful life to inspection. Do you have the impression he was shocked by what he found? See verses 17-18. You can't shock Christ. He knows it all already and he's seen exactly the same thing a few million times before! You might as well face facts.

Besides facing what you *are,* you'd better face what you *ought* to be, too. That's in verse 23. God looks for people who will honor and serve him "in spirit" (with all their hearts) and "in truth" (with a pure life). How different from that woman grasping vainly for happiness with her six lovers!

● **Take a good look at Christ.** Oh yes, the woman had known about him (25); but that made no difference to her. Now she met him, looked him in the eye, and heard his words. In the next couple of days we'll see what a difference that made.

Prayer

Lord Jesus, show me what I am really like. Then show me what You can make me. Amen.

Keynote

Life is fact, not fiction

Reapers Wanted!

Another social convention broken! "The disciples were amazed to find him talking with a *woman!*" (27). "It isn't *done,* you know!" All right, but if you're going to "reap" people for Jesus Christ you'll have to ignore certain ideas of what is or isn't done. You'll have to break through the prejudices of some narrow-minded Christians, too! Otherwise you'll never get *near* the people Christ wants you to reach.

Ready for reaping? Then let's think of:

● **The aim.** What had Christ done for the woman? Given her a bigger income? Improved her housing? Taught her better hygiene? *No!* Jesus knew these were important; but they were not what was crucial. Instead he brought her to himself (29), and made her face herself, gave her new life in her heart! You can help bring these gifts to those in need.

● **The method.** What was Christ's method? Not just "showing concern," or introducing her to a group. It was talking to her; telling her about God and about her life, and most of all about himself, Jesus Christ. There's no substitute!

● **The result.** To "finish a work" for God is food for your soul (34) — real, deep satisfaction. Your "wages"? A joy you'll find nowhere else (36).

Prayer

Lord, as I look at people around me, I know the fields are STILL ripe for harvest. Train me to be a reaper, for Your sake. Amen.

Keynote

She wasted no time (28). And you?

S-T-E-P-P-I-N-G Stones

Do you wish you had some actual *proof* that Christianity is true? Look at the people here, how certain they were about Christ. But they'd actually *seen* him, and his miracles. That made it easy.

● **"Now we know,"** said the Samaritans (42). Why? Because they'd seen Jesus for themselves.

● **"Then the father knew"** (53). Why? Because Christ had done a miracle. It doesn't seem fair.

But wait a minute! Did you notice that the Samaritans and the father got to that point by stages — by STEPS?

(a) The Samaritans. STEP 1: They heard what *the woman* said, and believed that much (39). STEP 2: They heard what Christ said, and believed more (41). STEP 3: They lived with Christ two days; then they really KNEW (42).

(b) The father. STEP 1: He heard what *others* said, and believed enough to come (47). STEP 2: He heard what *Christ* said, and believed that (50). STEP 3: He saw Christ's power work in his home; then he really KNEW (53).

Let the testimony of other Christians, and the words of the Bible, and your own experiences, be STEPPING STONES to a firmer faith!

Prayer

Lord, help me to believe what I've already seen and heard; then give me more when I'm ready for it. Amen.

Keynote

Just one step at a time.

Get Right and Stay Right!

● **The danger of going wrong.** In verse 14 Jesus suggests that in this case (not in every case, but in this case) the man had been sick because he had gone wrong. We're not told *how* he went wrong, but we do know it ruined his life for 38 years (5). The opposite is true, too. The best investment for mental and physical health is good, clean living.

● **The danger of staying wrong.** Jesus didn't ask that question in verse 6 just for something to say! There are people, and always have been, who don't *want* their lives put straight. Christ can give them a new life and set them on a new path, but there's not enough *spice* for them in "good, clean living" — not enough fun. Do you think this man gave a straight answer (7)? What is yours?

● **The danger of going wrong again.** What a warning the man got (14)! To go back to what you have been saved from can be utter disaster. The backlash will be worse next time, and the cure much harder or even impossible.

The Lord has all the power you could ever need to PUT you right and KEEP you right. All you have to do is *want* it.

Prayer

Lord, save me from tolerating wrong in my life, or trifling with it. Make me clean, and keep me clean, I pray. Amen.

Keynote

Everything comes to him who WANTS

Dead or Alive?

VERSE
OF THE WEEK
John 6:37

When we use the words "dead" and "living" we usually mean people who are physically dead or alive. But Jesus taught us that it is possible to be walking around and laughing and making money — and yet be dead inside! And that it's possible to get a *new kind of life* that makes the life you've been living up to now seem like just an empty shell. So look at these different people.

● **The dead people.** To look at, they're not much different from the living people. But what you see is all there is of them! Inside them is just a gray deadness. They don't know God; they've never taken new life from Jesus Christ (21). The end of verse 29 is their end, too.

● **The living people.** Outwardly they may look more or less the same. But look what Christ has given them (21) — *exactly the same spring of life that makes God himself what he is* (26)! There are a lot of these people around; are you one of them?

● **Dead people come alive.** Yes, right now it can happen! "The hour is coming, AND NOW IS, when" — what (25)? Just look at verse 24! You *hear,* you *believe,* you *trust* yourself to Christ, and what happens?

Prayer

O Christ, how can I live without this life? May I come alive today, and share Your life with others. Amen.

Keynote

Look alive!

You Be the Judge!

Look back at verses 21 to 24; Christ was making some pretty stupendous claims. Maybe you need some convincing. Well, you be the judge today, and listen while Christ calls four witnesses to the stand. Then make up your mind.

● **A human witness** (33). John the Baptist gave testimony that Jesus was God's Son. *There are many "human witnesses" today who will tell you the same thing.*

● **A visible witness** (36). A popular singer recently said Jesus was "some kind of crackpot." Study all that Jesus said and did and you'll be convinced that if anyone is a "crackpot," it must be the one who made such an accusation!

● **A divine witness** (37). Come to God through Jesus and you'll find him! Pray to God in Christ's name and you'll get answers! That's how God himself stands by Jesus Christ.

● **A written witness** (39). The more you read the Bible, the more sure you'll be that Jesus was really sent by God.

Then why don't some people believe in him? Not because they *can't* believe, but because they WON'T (40). Are you a "believer"?

Prayer

Father God, make people more honest as they think about Christ, and help them to believe in him. For his sake. Amen.

Keynote

Consider your verdict

Bread for the Hungry

This miracle is usually taken as an illustration of how we should be passing the Gospel to people who are "hungry" to know God. This is not wrong. But don't miss the *first* truth in this story, which is that *Jesus fed a crowd of hungry people with bread and fish!* Take it that way today.

● **Christ cares about the people's stomachs!** Sometimes it seems that the more "orthodox" Christians are, the less they care about whether people have enough to eat. This isn't right. Wherever people are hungry, it's our job to try to get food to them (5).

● **Christ cares about the poor supply!** It would take an array of computers to calculate how many distressed people are in the world — teeming in city slums, huddled in refugee camps, starving in famine-stricken areas, or made homeless by war. Forty dollars worth (7)? No, Philip; forty million dollars worth would not be enough! But still Christ cares.

● **Christ cares about the proper solution!** And what *is* the proper solution? For those who care to *do what they can* (9), however little it may seem. Small gifts have a way of getting multiplied (11)!

Prayer

O God, help all the needy people of this world. Use me to answer this prayer. For Jesus' sake. Amen.

Keynote

Let hand follow heart

How to Cope with Life

● **What you must expect.** The disciples didn't *ask* to be in a boat in the middle of a storm. Probably they'd have said they didn't deserve to have something like that happen to them. They had to learn — and *we* have to learn — that Christ has no intention of shielding us from the hard knocks of life. If a strong wind blows, the sea will rise (18) — for Christians and everyone else.

● **What you must tackle.** That must have been hard rowing (19). Christ doesn't want us to complain, but rather to come to grips with what he allows to come. Nor does he say, "There, there!" — and stop the wind blowing! He doesn't want us to be weak and spineless; tackling trouble bravely is one of the ways we become strong.

● **What you must remember.** First, the disciples learned that Christ could stride on top of the waves and cut his way through the wind. Nothing can defeat him or get *him* down. But notice carefully, he didn't say to them, "It is I, I will end the storm." He didn't even say, "I will get you safely to the shore." He said, *"It is I, do not be afraid"* (20). That was enough for them; it should be enough for us, too.

Prayer

Lord, forgive me if I've expected things to be easy. Give me the courage to face anything with You. Amen.

Keynote

Never alone

Priorities

What do you put first in life?

● **Do you pay more attention to the body than the soul?** That's what Christ is getting at in verse 26. Do you put more into a career than into serving Christ better? Is love of some "treasure" keeping you from complete commitment to Christ?

FIRST SELF-TEST. Answer this question honestly, in one sentence: What do you hope to achieve in life more than anything else? We'll evaluate your answer in a minute.

● **Do you pay more attention to this life than the next?** See verse 27. For example, which concerns you more: to give your children a good start *materially,* or to help them to know Christ?

SECOND SELF-TEST. Be honest, which is more likely to give you a sleepless night — a financial problem or a spiritual problem? Why?

Christ never underestimates man's need for physical sustenance and some material comfort. (See the note of two days ago.) But when we put these needs *above* our need and concern for him he sounds the alarm. Just as we need bread to stay alive, we also need the *True Bread,* Christ, to be really alive.

Prayer

Lord God, may I always put Christ first, others next, myself last. Amen.

Keynote

Are first things first?

Check Points on the Road to God

Why not find out how far you've come along the road that leads to God? Here are the check points:

● **I hear and learn from the Father.** Verse 45. *It means:* I read my Bible, hear preachers, read books, and so on, and God helps me understand what the Gospel really means.

● **I am drawn by the Father toward Christ.** Verse 44. *It means:* As I read, listen, and think, I feel more and more a desire inside me to know Jesus Christ for myself.

● **I make up my mind, and come to Christ.** Verse 45. This is my greatest moment of all. *It means:* By deliberate choice, I take Jesus Christ into my life.

● **I live by Jesus Christ, my bread of life.** Verse 48. *It means:* He is my "daily bread," my strength for each day, my daily guide on my road through life.

● **I am allowed to be with Jesus forever.** Verse 51. *It means:* At the end of this road, I'm welcomed into Christ's Kingdom in heaven.

A test question: Which point have I reached? What progress am I making toward the next one?

Prayer

Thank You, Father, that the road is so clearly marked. May I never get stuck, but always keep moving on. For Jesus' sake. Amen.

Keynote

On to glory!

What Is a Christian?

These verses seem difficult, don't they? But they're important, because they tell us the differences between a real Christian and a sham. You see, to be a Christian—

● **It's not enough to hear Christ's teaching.** Think about those "disciples" in verses 60, 64, 66. Did they hear? Did they commit themselves?

● **It's not enough to keep company with Christ.** What about that man in verses 70-71? He was one of Jesus' chosen workers.

No, these things are not enough. YOU MUST EAT HIS FLESH AND DRINK HIS BLOOD. Verse 53 could not be plainer, but what does it *mean*?

You must believe — believe that his flesh and blood were given for you when he died. Look back to verse 51. You must leave your sins at the cross with Jesus.

You must receive — receive Jesus Christ into your life. Jesus doesn't mean you *literally* eat his body (see verse 63). He means that you take him into yourself, and his life and yours become joined into one. This union between a believer and Christ is both a miracle and a mystery. It is in the Lord's Supper that this relationship is represented and enhanced. See verse 56.

Are you one with Christ? Are you a Christian?

Prayer

Lord Jesus, I take You into myself. I give You my heart and my life. May I live by Your strength today. Amen.

Keynote

Never the same again

Your Introduction to Daniel

The book of Daniel is a most unusual book.

Chapters 1-6 tell of the experiences of Daniel and his friends as they sought to be true to their God while in a pagan environment. The two main themes are:

(a) we owe our highest allegiance to God, not to human rulers;

(b) God is sovereign over kings and kingdoms and will judge their arrogance and wickedness. Each theme has special relevance for today.

Chapters 7-12 are composed of Daniel's visions. The author's message is sometimes difficult to discern because it is cloaked in symbolic language. In this second half of the book there is strong prophetic concentration on the Maccabean period (175-134 B.C.), to which most of the visions point.

However Biblical prophecy is two-dimensional, relating both to its own time and to the future. Seen in Christian perspective, the references to the Ancient of Days (7:9-10), and to the Son of Man coming on the clouds (7:13-14), surely apply to the Second Coming of Christ in Glory and to God's final judgment over evil in the world.

Daniel brings a message of hope for our time. Though evil rages, and governments pursue their selfish ways, driving us almost to despair, we can have hope. God himself will obtain ultimate victory through his Son Jesus Christ, King of kings.

Principles to Live By

"You've got to conform if you're going to get along," we're told, "otherwise you make everyone else feel uncomfortable. You have to 'stretch a point' now and then!" Daniel faced these temptations; we all do.

The temptations

"Don't look small!" — they'll think you're some kind of fanatic. "Don't jeopardize your future!" — in a high position you'll have a big influence for God; don't risk losing it! "Don't embarrass others!" — they won't understand anyway. "Don't be negative!" — people don't like a lot of "thou-shalt-nots."

The answer

Has two parts to it: (a) Purpose. A firm decision that no matter what, you will do what the Lord has shown you to be right (8). (b) Courtesy. This was one of the main ingredients in Daniel's character; it kept people friendly even when he had to take a stand (9).

The results

You are true to yourself. You're true to God. And the results may not be as disastrous as you expect!

Thought

How do you decide how far you can go before you dig in your heels?

Joint Operation!

Every good thing a Christian achieves is a "joint operation" between him and God. Today's story illustrates this.

Men standing up for God

They gave up some fine food and drink! Yes, from the king's own table! There was nothing wrong with the food itself, but it had to be avoided because of its associations (probably with idol worship).

They risked being expelled from their training course.

They staked their future on God's faithfulness (13). If God had let them down, they'd have looked foolish and been made to do as they were told.

God standing up for men

He gave them physical stamina (15). I assume their good health was a special gift from God in this case, not just the result of eating "plain food"! God honored their loyalty and stood by them.

He gave them mental brilliance (17). I've known cases of Christians with little education who have revealed a high level of intelligence and an ability to communicate, seemingly through simple association with Christ and God's Word.

Thought

Are Christians today recognized by non-Christians as being particularly "wise"?

Pray

that you may obey God closely in your day-to-day decisions.

Character Will Win

It's how a person reacts to unexpected events that shows what his character is really like. People who know God and people who don't know God often react differently. You have an example of that in the reactions of Nebuchadnezzar and Daniel.

Nebuchadnezzar — a man without God

He seemed to be completely in control of himself and of his life, but he had a gruesome dream, and what was inside came out! Unstable, superstitious, too. A man without God lacks the rocklike foundation to his life which a Christian can have. Vindictive. Taking out on his subordinates the insecurity inside himself — something you've probably seen happen. Unreasonable. Surprisingly enough, it's hard to act in a reasonable way under pressure, if you don't know God.

Daniel — a man with God

We have only a brief glimpse of Daniel, in verses 14-16. Enough to show him calm in an emergency, respectful to an enemy officer, sensible in tackling a dangerous situation. The opposite of Nebuchadnezzar!

Thought

When under pressure, do you tend to react like Nebuchadnezzar or like Daniel?

Pray

for a well-balanced personality, based on intimate contact with Christ.

Man of God in a Crisis

Today we find clear pointers on how a Christian should conduct himself in a crisis.

Encourage all to pray (17-18). This can easily be the one thing that's forgotten or minimized. In a critical situation it can seem impractical or a waste of precious time.

Seek light from God (18). Every crisis has an "interpretation" capable of being revealed by God.

Praise God (20) even while the crisis is still on!

Care for all in the situation (24), even those who don't share your faith in Christ.

View the situation through the character of God (20-23). To put it another way, think out what God's purpose in the critical situation may be, in the light of what you know about him.

Now think about Daniel's words to the King (27-30). There is a false humility when we pretend to give God credit for things which are due to our own studies or experience. This can be infuriating. But Daniel gives genuine credit to God for what he could never have done by himself. That makes sense.

Thought

What do you think is the main reason Daniel showed up so well in this whole set of circumstances?

Pray

that you may be capable of taking a lead when a crisis arises.

History on the Move

The "great image" (31) represented four world empires: Babylon ("the head of gold"), the Medes and Persians ("the chest and arms of silver"), Greece ("the hips and thighs of bronze"), and Rome ("the legs and feet of iron and clay"). During the fourth empire (Rome), God would set up his own Kingdom — a Kingdom to come from heaven and not from men (44-45). This Kingdom, in the end, would replace all the others. Has all this come true?

Great powers and human forces seem so "permanent" when we live with them. Yet they, too, have "feet of clay." One by one they deteriorate and fade, and one day the last of them will disappear. In place of them all, the Kingdom of Jesus Christ will find the whole earth (35)!

At first sight, what you read in your morning newspaper may not seem to tie in with your Bible reading, prayer, worship, or Christian fellowship. But if God is working in history, then his hand is moving history today — and in one sense history today is what you read in your paper and hear on the news.

Thought

What other cases are there in the Bible of God speaking through dreams? Does he still do it today?

Worship

God as Lord of lords and King of kings.

Living for God in a Pagan World

Don't be surprised and don't let it discourage you if you find that the majority of the people around you aren't Christians. It's not new, it's always been so; it was foretold by Jesus. Shadrach, Meshach and Abednego set a fine example of how to handle this situation.

They became involved in the life of their society. They didn't isolate themselves from people. As far as they could be, they were loyal to the existing system, and even reached high positions. Their influence must have been great.

They drew the line on a question of principle. "The idol is nothing but wood overlaid with gold, to bow down means nothing; it can do no harm!" That's how they might have reasoned. Why do you think they decided to take a stand? (Exodus 20:4-5 may help). There comes a point where you can no longer influence people by going along with their way of life.

They left the outcome in the hands of God. Not reluctantly, or fatalistically, but joyfully and triumphantly (17-18).

Thought

Verse 8 is true to life. Why do certain people tend to hate those who love and serve God? What should the Christian's attitude be to those who accuse him?

Ask God

for the kind of courage that he gave to these three men.

Moment of Truth

It would have been just too bad if they'd been bluffing all the time — if they hadn't really meant what they said. Now it's the moment of truth, the king takes them at their word — they must see it through.

The king himself, in verse 28, testified as to how far they were prepared to go. For Shadrach, Meshach and Abednego it was better to die than to deny their Lord.

Wouldn't it have been terrible if they'd staked their all on God, only to find that he let them down or didn't even exist? God must either show himself now or suffer great disrepute. He showed himself!

The remarkable thing is not so much the miracle itself (that their lives were saved) as that their God was with them, even in the fire!

The king had to acknowledge that God was with them. And many are like him today. They need to see it as it is, not just to hear "Jesus-talk." Then they can acknowledge that God is alive.

Thought

Can you give an example, from your own experience, of a way in which a Christian today may have to suffer for his faithfulness to Christ?

Pray

that the way Christians live may show everyone that Jesus is alive.

How Great Is Great?

VERSE OF THE WEEK
Daniel 4:3

The Bible nowhere says it's wrong for one person to have authority over another. Parents may control their children, employers may direct their employees, kings may rule their subjects. Revolutionaries who want to abolish all authority are quite wrong. The Bible says it is God who puts people into positions of authority — even if they sometimes aren't worthy of it.

Now think about greatness.

Human greatness

It has its value. This is clear from the beginning of Nebuchadnezzar's dream. Notice the good functions performed by the tall tree (11-12), and think out what each of them means. A godly person in a position of power can do immense good.

It has its limitations. Interesting, isn't it, that for all the king's power, a simple dream could make him "terrified" and "alarmed" (5)? Without faith in God, power can be a very precarious thing.

Divine greatness

The story we begin today is about how Nebuchadnezzar learned that God is as he is described in verses 2 and 3. Being in touch with God makes all the difference in the world to a leader.

Thought

What "power" do you have? How can you best use it for God?

Pray

for those in authority, all over the world.

40

God's Strange Ways

No psychiatrists in those days! Yet Nebuchadnezzar was to be plunged into terrible mental illness, and the amazing thing is — God ordered it that way! Perhaps there are equally mysterious problems in your own experience.

Nevertheless, the point is God had a purpose in it. He had spoken in other ways; now he proposed drastic measures. Look:

God used quiet reasoning. Nebuchadnezzar was "high and mighty." How to bring him down? We've seen three ways God showed his power to Nebuchadnezzar (one each in Chapters I, 2 and 3). But he paid no attention, and carried on in his own way.

God gave a final warning. Through his servant Daniel, God gave a last call to Nebuchadnezzar to change his ways (verse 27). God has many different ways of doing this. Usually it's some event that brings us up short and forces us to think.

God sent a terrible tragedy. Nebuchadnezzar would become mad, be driven from society, act like an animal. Picture his wife and his family in their distress. Yet it was the only way God could get through — apparently it worked!

Thought

What did Nebuchadnezzar need to learn (17, and end of 25)? What difference would this make in his life?

Pray

that you may learn God's lessons one by one as they come.

Self-glorification

Pride, or self-glorification, is a sin God finds repulsive. Yet it's one of the most common sins, even among Christians.

It can take two forms. (a) *It can be expressed.* Nebuchadnezzar wasn't ashamed to boast: "Isn't this great Babylon, which I've built by my own mighty power?" We find this kind of talk very unpleasant; for that reason most people are more subtle about their boasting. (b) *It can be implied.* Remember how the Pharisee in one of Jesus' parables said: "God, I thank You that I'm not like other men — I fast twice a week..." He used a prayer to parade himself! We devise all kinds of ways to let others know what fine people we are or what good things we've done!

It's an attitude of mind. If God objects to the presumptuous things we say, It's only because they betray the proud mind that lies behind them. So it's no good just guarding against saying certain kinds of things. We need a humble heart.

It's a dangerous condition. If we won't humble ourselves, God may find it necessary to do it for us (32).

Thought

Christian workers and organizations send out newsletters to help people pray for their work. Do they sometimes fall into the sins of pride and boasting? How can they avoid this?

Give

to Jesus all credit for whatever is good in your life.

A Changed Man

Changed, yes — but what a hard process! How much easier if Nebuchadnezzar had submitted to God freely, while he had the chance! In any case, God touched him, and he was never the same again.

His attitude to God was changed

Like so many people, the farthest he had come so far was to pay God nice compliments — nod his head to him politely, as it were. Now it all became personal, as you see from verse 34. His heart is bowed before God.

His attitude to himself was changed

The last part of verse 37 shows that Nebuchadnezzar's attitude to himself is changed — he's no longer obsessed with his own power or infallibility. He's no longer looking down at the city he'd built, but...(34)?

His attitude to his people was changed

Everyone in the kingdom would benefit by the change. The change was "for the glory of my kingdom," he said (36). I think that meant "for the good of my people," and that he'd treat them now as persons, not as property.

Thought

Nebuchadnezzar's reason returned when he became rightly related to God. How far can a person be truly "rational" if he doesn't know God?

Pray

for all who are putting personal ambition before the glory of God.

Characters in the Story

Belshazzar

We've jumped 25 years since the last chapter; Nebuchadnezzar is long dead. While his father Nabonidus (the real king) is away, Belshazzar is reveling as king. What's he like?

On the outside: brash and self-confident, popular, surrounded by his friends, contemptuous of God, sneering at followers of the Lord, worldly, sensuous, materialistic — all this comes out in verses 1-4. He has many like him today.

On the inside: a different story! His personal crisis in verses 5-9 shows him to be insecure, panicky, and troubled by a bad conscience. All well covered; but ready to break out when his self-sufficient world is pierced.

Not an attractive character. But there are others in the story.

Daniel

Do you imagine it was easy for Daniel to be true to God in the situation we read about today? I doubt it! Yet he was faithful and consistent and well known as a godly man.

The Queen

Or more likely the "queen-mother." She watched Daniel, saw his life — and knew where to turn for help!

Thought

What do you learn about the Lord from this story?

Ask

the Lord to help you live a consistent, attractive Christian life wherever you may be.

Portrait of a Fool

Daniel deliberately holds up a mirror to Belshazzar: "Now just stop and have a look at yourself!" he seems to say. I wonder what Belshazzar saw!

Did he see his four sins?

What were they? Look in verses 22-23:

He had not cultivated a humble heart.

He had put himself before the Lord.

He had given himself up to a godless life.

He had worshiped things instead of the one true God.

Did he see his one great sin?

Those words at the end of verse 23 are some of the finest Daniel ever uttered: "The God in whose hand is your breath, and whose are all your ways, you have not honored." For all practical purposes, Belshazzar had left God out of his life. Yet without God he could not draw another breath or walk another step.

And there was no excuse for Belshazzar. Why not (22)?

Thought

Dare you look at yourself in the same mirror? Have you avoided Belshazzar's mistakes? Have you honored the God who holds your breath in his hand?

Worship

the Most High God, the Lord of heaven and earth.

"Weighed and Found Wanting"

Mene, Tekel and *Peres* (plural Parsin) are names of weights, or coins, each less than the one before. So it's "Mina (dollar) mina, shekel, and half-shekels." The king's "value" is dropping to nothing. But more: the words are a riddle, with a double meaning. *Mina* literally means "number," which explains verse 26, *Tekel* or *shekel* means "weigh" (27); and *Peres* means "divide," while the word for Persian is written exactly the same (28)! All this Daniel explains.

For Belshazzar it's a message of doom. No word for him like that in 4:27 to Nebuchadnezzar. He's gone too far, it's the end. How will he react?

Belshazzar's amazing unconcern. No sign of anxiety now, no repentance, no night of prayer. What does he do (29)? He shows how little he cares about God's message by making Daniel third ruler of a kingdom God has just said is finished!

Daniel's amazing faithfulness. It took courage to tell this brash king his kingdom was finished, his life worthless, his armies defeated! But courteously Daniel did it.

Thought

Too many courteous Christians lack courage to speak frankly. And too many Christians "say what they think" without love or politeness.

Pray

for the right combination of outspokenness and Christian courtesy.

Keep Praying!

Apart from God working in people's hearts, human nature does produce friction and jealousy between people. You see it in almost every office or school, in fact, wherever people are thrown closely together. Jealousy drove Daniel's associates to seek to destroy him. He faced lies (7 — "All the presidents"? see verse 2!), spying (11), prejudice — probably racial (13), and slander (13). He responded by utter loyalty to the king — and to God — and by a life so pure and trustworthy that even his enemies admitted "he was faithful, and no error or fault was found in him" (4)! Now how would you answer if someone asked you these questions?

"How can Daniel have been right to accept such a high position under a pagan king?"

"For the sake of a mere 30 days, wouldn't Daniel have been wiser to obey the king's order?"

"Wasn't Daniel making a show of his religion by praying at an open window?"

"Wouldn't Daniel have been wiser to pray out of sight? That way, he could have stayed true to God without getting into trouble."

"If those men hated him so intensely mustn't Daniel have been hard to live with?"

Pray *for infinite patience when people make themselves your enemies.*

One of God's Well-wishers

Darius — you must have met someone like him. Not a Christian, but sufficiently attracted by Christians to be a well-wisher to God's servants; sometimes even helping in God's work. As we analyze Darius, see if there is someone you know who fits the picture.

He's not a committed believer himself. Darius still had a lot of personal pride (7,9).

He's attracted to people who serve the Lord, recognizes their trustworthiness, likes their character (14).

He appreciates God, but from a distance! He's "your God," not "my God" (16,20).

He's developing a conscience. He worries about Daniel, spends the night fasting (18).

He tries to help God's cause as he's able (24,26).

He's slowly making progress toward God. Gradually he learns, slowly his heart changes (27).

There is no record that Darius was converted to the Lord by Daniel's witness. But he did come a step closer.

Thought

Should Darius have agreed to Daniel being punished? Or should he have pronounced the whole thing a trick and let Daniel go? What would you have done?

Pray

for anyone you know who is slowly finding out about Christ.

Daniel's Vision

(To better understand today's passage, first read verses 1-8. We're reading part of a dream or vision God gave to Daniel.)

A vision of heaven

(9-12) This vision encouraged Daniel by showing him that the great kings and armies that were grappling for control of the world were not the whole story. In heaven there was another throne and another king — "the Ancient of Days," the Mighty God. Earthly kings were cruel and unfair, but the heavenly King is completely pure, completely just (9). And he will have the last word (10-11)!

A vision of earth

(13-14) Our eyes now turn to the future, for a great message of hope. One day unjust powers of this world will fade away, and make way for a new Kingdom, pure and good and indestructible (14).

And who will be the king in this new Kingdom? Who will at last bring unity and peace to this world? The one in verse 13, none other than the Messiah, Jesus Christ (John 1:51).

Thought

Who are the real bosses in your country? Big business— giant corporations — trade unions — politicians — the military? What does today's passage have to say about them?

Thank

God for his promise of a new and better world.

"A Man Greatly Beloved"

Let's see what in this story made Daniel particularly "beloved" by God.

Confidence in God's Word. Everything began while Daniel was reading God's Word through the prophet Jeremiah (2). He found the book had something to say about his own day and situation! He believed it, and took action.

Confession of unfaithfulness. Here's an important idea. He didn't point to the sins of "other people." We know what a fantastically good-living man Daniel was; yet he said, "We have sinned and done wrong and acted wickedly and rebelled" (5) — "We have not listened to Thy servants the prophets" (6) — "To us, O Lord, belongs confusion of face" (8)! It will not do to talk about the sins of hippies, or criminals, or governments, or capitalists, or Communists, or others in the church. It is "our sins" that Christians should be confessing — sins we share with all humanity.

Comfort from a loving God. Confession paves the way for more sensitivity and understanding (22). God's first answer to Daniel's prayer was to help him see more clearly what was happening, and to give him strength to live through it.

Thought

What sins of your society are you especially conscious of?

Confess

these sins to God; ask for his forgiveness and help.

Catching the Vision

The background

The vision Daniel so badly needed came while he was "mourning" (2). Why was he mourning? Perhaps for the same reason as in chapter 9, verse 5. Or maybe he had received discouraging news of the Jews who had already returned to Jerusalem. Be that as it may, we're wide open for new visions of God when we are deeply and personally concerned, especially about others.

The vision

An angel? Maybe. But some Bible teachers think that Daniel was granted a vision of Jesus Christ himself. Did it occur to you how similar this vision is to Paul's vision of Christ on the road to Damascus? The truth is that the only way you can see God is to see him in Jesus.

The effects

(a) Terror for the by-standers, even though they didn't actually see the figure. Did they perhaps feel something present?

(b) Awe for God's servant. He wasn't crushed, but he was almost overwhelmed. Let's never lose our ability to be overcome with wonder at the presence of God.

Thought

Can you figure out the meaning of each part of the description in verses 5 and 6?

Pray

that you may always have a "vision" of Christ and his will for your life.

The Part We Can Play

We have only been "dipping" into these later chapters of Daniel. They deal with God's plans for the nations of Daniel's day, and look ahead to the coming of Christ. You might read the complete chapters for yourself; you will sense something of God's great working in history.

Daniel's nation was occupied, the people scattered, the land barren. All credit to him, he doesn't retreat into a shell of self-pity, but boldly prays to God for his country.

This is the right thing to do. When a nation is in a time of crisis, or when evil is rampant or society in chaos, the Christians, with one heart and soul, should pray that God's love and power may break in. Miracles can happen.

Notice two things Daniel did:

(a) *He "set his mind to understand" (12).* For us, this means looking faithfully into God's Word, and into the situation in our nation, and fitting the two together.

(b) *He "humbled himself before God" (12).* As we saw in our passage of two days ago, it won't do to criticize "them" — it's *our* sinfulness we must confess.

The answers to our prayers may be delayed (13) but they will surely come (14,19)!

Thought

What changes would you like to see in your nation in the next five years?

Turn

these ideals into prayer, asking God to make them come true. Then be sure to vote!

Your Introduction to 1 Peter

This letter was written by one of Jesus' three closest followers to the scattered Christians of northern and western Asia Minor. It is full of doctrinal and practical teaching for the Christian. Much of it is in metaphorical terms: *babies, stones, race, priesthood, shepherd, flock, lion.*

Watch especially for some main themes:

● **God's people.** Their privileges, function in the world, suffering and sympathy, unity and destiny.

● **Jesus Christ.** His care and kindness, patience and example, suffering and self-denial, death and resurrection, glory and Lordship.

● **Warnings.** About returning to the pre-Christian life, doing wrong, having to give an account to God, failing in love to fellow Christians, retaliation under persecution, hindrances to prayer, self-seeking, pride, and the devil.

● **Suffering.** Peter has much to say about suffering, trials, and tribulation. Much of his insight comes to us, no doubt, as a result of his own experience as an apostle. Especially helpful are his teachings about the positive results and necessary function of suffering in the life of a Christian.

Let's Read the Will

"Someone has left you a fortune!" Such good news (12) is true if you are a Christian (2). The fortune is an inheritance (4), salvation (5,9), glory (7).

What does the Bible say about it?

● Is it based on merit or mercy; birth or achievement (3)? See also verse 23.

● Can you have it right now (4,5)?

● On what grounds can you positively look forward to it? Three answers in verses 3 to 5.

● Why does God keep you waiting for it (7)?

● What part can you have right now (8,9)?

● What was the particular task of the prophets mentioned in verses 10 to 12?

● What have you to say to those who:

(a) only want a good time?

(b) always complain about rising prices?

(c) are victims of the rat race?

(d) view the future with trepidation?

Note Peter's *fleeting* reference to his readers' original *earthly* state, and his *emphasis* on their *spiritual* state (1,2).

Pray

that Christians may show a greater love for the One who has left them a fortune in his will.

Keynote

"Kept...for you...who...are guarded"

Peculiar or Godly?

VERSE OF THE WEEK
1 Peter 2:20

What does the word *holy* (15) bring to your mind? Peculiar words ("thou," "ye")? Peculiar dress (black robes)? Stained-glass windows? We'd probably do better to think of a Christian truck driver in over-alls in a roadside diner.

Peter tells us that *holy* means *godlike* (15-16), through Christ (18,21). We may look forward eagerly to the fortune that awaits us (13). We must recognize and reverence God as our Father (14,17).

Peter exhorts us to remember how unholy we once were (14,18); to realize that we have been brought to God at such cost to Christ (19) and such power from God (21) and his Word (23-25); and that he wants us earnestly to love other Christians (22).

Think ● **How can you be an example of holiness in:**

● **crowded shopping areas?**

● **family quarrels?**

● **watching TV?**

● **Sunday worship?**

Pray

that God will show you how to live a godly life in an ungodly world.

Keynote

"You shall be holy, for I am holy"

Be a Brick!

Here are a number of metaphors. Each suggests something about the Christian life. Each reminds us that Christians belong to one another.

- **Babies in God's family** (2-3; see also verses 9-10).

How do you grow up? What incentives are mentioned?

- **Bricks in God's house** (4-5a; see also verses 6-8).

What gives security to bricks and offense to former builders?

- **Priests in God's temple** (5b; also verse 9).

What is their special function? On what do they depend?

- **Citizens of God's nation** (9-10).

Why and how does God make citizens? Spiritual sacrifices (5) mentioned in the New Testament include prayer, praise, evangelism, and material gifts to the ministry or to the poor.

Each of these metaphors suggests that Christians have a corporate life and a responsibility in the church.

In your relationship with other church members:

Question

- **Is there any malice, guile, insincerity, envy or slander (1)?**
- **Are you maturing spiritually?**
- **What deeds of God do you declare (9)?**

Keynote

"Once...no people, but now...God's people"

Good Citizens

The early Christians were accused of being *unpatriotic and atheistic,* because they would not call the emperor "Lord," nor acknowledge the Roman gods; *unsociable,* because they did not attend cruel sports or idolatrous feasts; *immoral,* because they held "love feasts" of their own; and *haters of mankind* because of their indifference to worldly ways and standards. What are the accusations today? Their answer was good deeds (12) as well as Gospel preaching. So must ours be.

● **Self-denial** (11). Remembering we are citizens of heaven, we are to abstain from the worship of wealth and fame, self-assertiveness, self-pity, quarreling and jealousy. Anything else?

● **Good living** (12). "Good" means lovely, fine, attractive. This is one of the best arguments for Christianity. Whom do you know who sets an example of this?

● **Loyal citizenship** (13-17). Though the government has no rightful control over opinions, God has ordained governments for law and order (Romans 13:1-4). Are we careful about income tax returns, customs, fares, public and private property, highway regulations, fair wages and hard work?

● **Verse 16: Free from the bondage of sin, Satan and public opinion, to do God's will.**

Pray

Lord, make me a good citizen both of heaven and of my country.

Keynote

"So that...they may see"

Don't Boss the Boss

The following was overheard in a coffee shop at lunch hour. "My boss is an absolute pig." "My boss is a great guy." "My boss is neither." Peter has a word especially for the first of these employees. We owe *proper respect* even to an overbearing boss because —

● **It is our duty** (18). The Bible does not theorize about a classless society. It demands submission to and respect for authority. Not even petty tyranny on the boss' part is sufficient cause for rudeness, slackness, indifference to instructions, or poor quality work.

● **It pleases God** (19-21). In enduring injustice, cultivate a sense of God's presence ("mindful of God") and "approval" (literally, "God says 'thank you' ").

● **It is following Christ's example** (21-23). See Luke 23:33-37. A Muslim was led to Christ through reading the words, "Father, forgive them."

● **It is fulfilling Christ's purpose** (24-25). It is an expression of dying to sin and living to righteousness (24); and of faith in Christ's care and provision (25).

Pray

for yourself in terms of the example of Christ recorded in five phrases in verses 22-23.

Keynote

"Follow in his steps"

A Pattern for the Home

a) For wives only (1-6). "Your beauty should reside not in...but in..." (NEB). There is no excuse here for a Christian woman to be dowdy. Her beauty should not depend on an expensive hair-do, sparkling jewelry and a beautiful dress, but on "the ageless beauty of a gentle and quiet spirit" (4, TEV), undaunted trust in God, and recognition of the husband's authority (5-6). Test yourself...

- **Are you more occupied with Christ than with your outward appearance?**
- **How much time do you spend in Bible reading and prayer compared with getting dressed?**

b) For husbands only (7). There is nothing about ruling here. Are we considerate in:

- **asking her what sort of day she's had?**
- **making our conversation interesting?**
- **doing our full share with the children?**
- **treating her gently (7b)?**
- **sharing her Christian interests and experiences (7c)?**
- **praying with her (7b)?**

c) For all (8-12). What should be our *attitude* toward fellow Christians, ourselves, our enemies? What about our *words*?

that God will create more homes which will be centers of Christian love, joy, peace, witness and work.

Giving an Answer

Persecuted Christians are sometimes asked the secret of their endurance.

"Always be prepared" (15) to answer inquiries. Bad moods are fatal. Verse 15 tells us to answer:

- **Intelligently** "make a defense"

- **Personally** "in you"

- **Modestly** "with gentleness"

- **Respectfully** "with reverence"

Verses 19-20. About four explanations of these verses have been attempted, and all of them have snags. We know that Christ existed and worked in Old Testament days before his human birth. Could these verses mean that, by his Spirit, through Noah, he had preached to the people of Noah's day, doomed by their own disobedience to judgment by the flood unless they repented?

Some interpret the "spirits in prison" here and the "sons of God" in Genesis 6:2,4 as fallen angels. But it is more likely that Genesis 6 refers to marriage between two human groups — godly and ungodly.

Verse 21

"Baptism, which corresponds to this, now saves you." Not the physical act, but what it stands for — cleansing from sin and a rising to a new life with Christ.

Prayer

Lord, keep me alert to answer questions about the hope and faith you have given me.

A Call to Arms

VERSE
OF THE WEEK
Peter 4:12-13

In our permissive society Christians need to be well-armed with right ideas (1). We have:

● **An example (1a).** In his human body and nature Christ resisted temptation; renounced self-will; depended on God; suffered tiredness, hunger, scorn, slander, disappointment, pain.

● **An exhortation (1b).** We must have the same attitude.

● **An experience(1c).** We shall then stop living a sinful life, no longer be ruled by bodily demands, and find ourselves freed to do God's will.

What if we then hanker after our former permissive ways (3)? What about our former companions (4-5)?

Verse 6. The most likely interpretation seems to be: "That is why the good news of salvation was preached (in their lifetime) to those who were going to die. For though their bodies would be given the death penalty, like anyone else, they could still be alive in the spirit, as God is" (Living Bible, footnote).

Pray

that Christians, like their Master, may find such liberty, fulfillment and delight in God's will that they will gladly give up self-will.

Keynote

"Arm yourselves"

Love and Happiness

a) Show deep love to Christians (7-11).

Are you willing to overlook Christians' faults (8)? Could you make more use of your home (9)? What is your special ability in the church (10)? What use do you make of it? What is your motivation (10-11)?

b) Find deep happiness in suffering as a Christian (12-19).

Suffering is to be expected by a Christian as a part of life, as a test of his faith (12), and as part of his oneness with Christ (13).

It looks as if the faithful Christian can't lose (14)! But verses 14 to 19 are full of warning. We must make sure our sufferings are *"for the name of Christ"* and not for our own folly and sin (14-16; see 2:20 and 3:17). Christians as well as unbelievers are under judgment (17-18). It is suffering *"according to God's will"* that warrants trust in God's vindication (19).

Verse 7a. As a thousand years is like a day to God, the end of the world is near and our own death very near.

Verse 7b. Keep a cool head. Learn self-control. Keep praying.

Prayer

for your church along the lines of verses 10 and 11 but in your own words.

Keynote

"That God may be glorified"

The Welfare Church

The idea of God's people being his flock is familiar both in the Old Testament and in the Gospels. Why did Peter have special reason to use it? (See John 21:15-17.)

● **The shepherds** (1-3). What are their duties and dangers? (Two answers for each — one from each of verses 2 and 3.)

● **The sheep** (2-3,5). Their tasks are to feed on what is provided (2), and follow the good example (3) and instruction of the shepherds (5). Which does your church need more: better preachers in the pulpit or better reactions from the listeners?

● **The Head Shepherd** (4). He has delegated the care of the flock to others. He will one day return to it with rewards for good work. Note: The word "clothe" in verse 5 is the same as for "gird" in John 13:4-5. Humility was an attractive garment on the Lord Jesus and it should be on every Christian. Humility is:

serviceable ("Wear the over-all of humility in serving each other" — 5b, Phillips);

comfortable ("God...gives grace to the humble");

becoming (What better attitude can men adopt "under the mighty hand of God"? — 6).

Pray for better and more humble leaders, preachers and hearers in the churches.

Keynote Humble yourselves

God Has the Answer

How much do we know in experience of:

● **God's antidote to worry** (7). A statement and command. Have we sufficiently realized that worry can be a sin?

● **God's antidote to the devil** (8-9). What attitude do we take toward ourselves (8); the devil; our faith; our fellow believers (9)? At what particular times may we need to resist the devil today?

● **God's antidote to self-pity** (9-10). Briefly summarize the teaching of 1 Peter on:

suffering (2:19-21; 3:14,17; 4:1,13-16,19)

the glory of Christ (1:11,21; 3:22; 4:11)

the Christian's future share in glory (4:13; 5:1,4,10)

Verse 13: "She" may be Peter's wife or more likely a sister church. "Babylon" may be taken literally or may refer to Rome, for which Christians used Babylon as a nickname.

Pray

for suffering Christians in the words of verses 10 and 11.

Keynote

"Eternal glory"

Your Introduction to Proverbs

"The Wise Man" in ancient Biblical times exercised a ministry second only to those of the prophet and the priest. It was his duty to translate the great principles which emerged from the Law and the preaching of the prophets into terms of everyday life and experience.

Solomon was, of course, not a wise man in the fully accepted sense of the term, but he was obviously a collector and indeed a coiner of proverbs, and no doubt contributed largely to the collection which he edited, and which we are about to read.

The *Psalms* equip us, as it were, with a telescope through which we may scan the greatness of God and the infinite variety of his work in nature, history and personal experience. The *Proverbs,* on the other hand, furnish us with a microscope which shows us the motives and manners, often devious and sometimes unrecognized, which color and influence human conduct.

This is a broad distinction and, of course, must not be pressed too far. For a proverb will often bring us down to earth, while a psalm may lift us up to heaven. It is in the *Psalms* that we learn more about God, and the *Proverbs* teach us most about man.

Choosing and Refusing

"The fear of the Lord is the beginning of knowledge" (7). It is said that a good sailor never loses his fear of the sea. To the end of his days he will regard it with awe and respect; and it is this deep sense of reverence for God which will set a man on the path of true wisdom and understanding.

● **Reject not** (8). Current attitudes encourage us, especially if we are young people, to regard with disfavor and suspicion any advice reaching us from parents and older friends! Not all such advice is sound, of course; but more often than not it is, since it stems from much greater experience, and at least it deserves to be listened to with attention and respect.

● **Consent not** (10). The other secret of wisdom is to recognize and refuse the voice of temptation, however attractively it is disguised. This requires courage, because sometimes to resist it will isolate us from other people who want us to join them (14) in what we know to be sinful and wrong.

Does this sound somewhat negative? Perhaps it is; but remember that in life, as in photography, a sharp negative is necessary if you want a clearly defined positive.

Prayer

Lord, give me the wisdom to know the difference between good and evil, and the courage always to choose the good and refuse the evil.

Keynote

"The fear of the Lord"

PROVERBS 2:1-15

True Wisdom

It is difficult to find a precise definition for the word *"wisdom"* which appears so often in this book. Sometimes it is almost personified, and some have equated it with the Holy Spirit. It is probably more exact to say that it is meant to represent *the knowledge of God (5) and his will.* In these verses we learn three things about it.

● **It has to be sought by man** (1-5). If you were told that your garden contained "hidden treasures" (4), wouldn't you dig up every inch of it? The knowledge of God is the greatest treasure anyone can find because it brings with it eternal life (John 17:3). How important that we should search for it with all our heart!

● **It has to be given by God** (6-9). We can only "discover" God as he reveals himself to us. He has done this in nature, in the Bible, and supremely, of course, in the Lord Jesus Christ. See 2 Corinthians 4:4.

● **It has to be applied to life** (10-15). To say that we know God, and to continue "to walk in the ways of darkness" (13) is, of course, a complete contradiction. Knowing him should keep us from sin in every shape and form. Look at 8:13 where we read, "The fear of the Lord" (and that is the beginning of wisdom) *"is hatred of evil."*

Prayer

Lord, may the knowledge and love of You keep me from every evil way.

Keynote

"The knowledge of God" (5)

Watch Out!

● **The danger of social immorality.** The rather vague warnings of yesterday lead today into the more sharply defined danger of immorality. It would seem that the evil practice of Solomon in marrying foreign, pagan women (1 Kings 11:1) had become common in Israel, and that these women, with their much laxer views on marriage, had become a deadly source of corruption. Such women would think nothing of forsaking the original partner of their marriage, or of "forgetting" the solemn vows they had taken before God (17).

● **The danger of spiritual idolatry.** Some view this passage as a parable of the country's "marriage" to God and their "adultery" in the worship of idols. Jeremiah in fact uses the same Hebrew phrase "the companion of her youth" for a passage in which he reproves the Jews for their unfaithfulness to God (Jeremiah 3:4).

In this spiritual sense, verse 17 is a solemn challenge to the backslider. Have we forsaken the Lord who guided and befriended us in the difficult problems we faced as young Christians? Have we forgotten the vows and promises to be faithful which we made in the first enthusiasm of our love for him?

Prayer

From immorality in all its forms, and from spiritual idolatry, good Lord, deliver me.

Keynote

"The friend of my youth"

Examining Your Life

These are principles for truly successful and happy Christian living, and we can hardly do better than test our lives by the standards laid down here.

● **Is yours a sanctified life** (1-4)? God's law and will should constantly be in our minds and hearts, governing our every thought, word and action.

● **Is yours a guided life** (5-6)? God wants to lead us in "the paths of righteousness" (Psalm 23:3). The secret of enjoying his guidance is seen in these verses: confidence in his power and willingness to lead; reliance upon his wisdom and not upon our own frail human understanding; obedience to his will insofar as he reveals it to us.

● **Is yours a consecrated life** (7-10)? The thought here seems to be that the Lord wants the first claim upon our gifts and talents. He asks us to put them at his disposal, so that he may use them in his service.

● **Is yours a disciplined life** (11-12)? The only way to make progress in the classroom or in sports is to be willing to have our faults "corrected." God wants to use his Word, our own experience, and often the advice of others, to discipline us and make us better Christians.

Prayer

Lord, make me into the sort of Christian who "finds favor" with You.

Keynote

He leads and he loves

Precious Treasure

Bearing in mind that "wisdom" stands for the fear and knowledge of God, we see that it is compared here to some of the most precious things known to man — silver, gold, jewels (14-15); and man's attitude toward it may be summed up as follows:

● **Found** (13-20). First, he must make the discovery for himself. He must find the treasure (15) and reach the tree (18). This is a personal, individual experience which comes to all who make Christ their Savior and Friend.

● **Enjoyed** (21-26). Those who come to know God through Jesus Christ find that he can give them security (23) and confidence (26) which are to be found nowhere else.

● **Shared** (27-32). A gentle (30) and generous (27-28) attitude toward other people will be a way of showing them what the Lord means to us, and perhaps of encouraging them to make the great discovery for themselves.

● **Used** (32-35). The knowledge of God should make a marked difference in our own personal character. Notice the adjectives in these verses: "upright" (32), "righteous" (33), "humble" (34), "wise" (35). Are those the kinds of words which other people would use to describe us?

Prayer

Lord, grant that my whole life may be enriched and blessed through my knowledge of Your love and power.

Keynote

"Better than...silver" (14)

Learning to Walk

Anyone who is learning to walk is liable to make one or both of two errors. He is apt to stumble (12) and he is apt to stray (27). Verses 12 and 27 are really intended to keep people from making these two particular mistakes.

● **Stumbling.** If you have ever watched a small child learning to walk, you will know how dependent he is upon someone to hold (13) and someone to lead (11). In the same way many pitfalls await the Christian, and if he is to avoid these, he must learn to rely completely upon his Guide and Instructor.

● **Straying.** As we continue in the Christian life, and as we perhaps grow a little more confident and sure of ourselves, we come to the temptation to stray "into the path of the wicked" (14). How can we avoid doing this? First, the *heart* must be right (23), for it is the source and spring of all action; then the *eyes* (25) must "look directly forward" (Hebrews 12:1-2) toward the goal we are trying to reach; and finally the *feet* (26) will go where they should.

Look at verse 18. It suggests that the farther we go along the right way, the brighter it becomes. In other words, the *closer* we keep to the Lord, the *clearer* becomes the course he wants us to take.

Prayer

"*Lead me, Lord, in thy righteousness...make thy way straight before me" (Psalm 5:8).*

Keynote

The closer, the clearer

Three Portraits

Three kinds of people are described in these verses, and we will consider each in turn.

● **The sluggard** (9). Have you ever seen an ant taking time off or asleep? It always seems to be occupied in some important business, always energetic and active. So, says the writer, we must be on our guard against laziness and too much sleep. We must find out just what we need to be at our best physically, spiritually and mentally.

● **The sinner** (12-19). Do you notice how, in these verses, almost every part of the body seems to be infected? The eyes, the feet, the fingers (13), the tongue, the hands (17), the heart (18). This is because sin is like a disease, beginning in the heart, at the center of our personality, and spreading to every corner of our life, affecting all we think and say and do.

● **The son** (20-24). A good son is guided by his father's instructions; and that, too, ought to be the mark of God's children. His commandments must be closely kept (21-22) and constantly used (23). Keep them as you would keep a precious jewel, close to your heart; use them as you would use a flashlight, to show you the way along a darkened street or passage.

Prayer

O Lord, help me to learn from the busy energy of the ant how to be actively engaged in Your service.

Keynote

"Go to the ant..."

Wisdom Speaks

In this passage Wisdom is not regarded as a thing, but as a person (12). Great interpreters of Scripture have, not unwisely, identified Wisdom with Christ himself (cf. 8:22 ff. with Colossians 1:15 ff.). The knowledge of God has passed into the person of God. One of his greatest attributes has become personified, and speaks.

● "I was..." (30). Genesis 1:26 suggests that there was more than one person present at the time of the Creation: ("Let *us* make..."). Many have thought that this points to the presence of God the Son as an active agent in the Father's creative work.

● "I have..." (14). To have him living within us by his Holy Spirit is to have wisdom and strength. These things are inseparable from him. To have the wind is to have power. To have the sun is to have light and warmth. To have Christ is to have wisdom and strength.

● "I fill..." (21). These verses are full of the wonderful things that are promised to those who possess Christ, pictured again in the now familiar symbols of riches (18) and fruit (19).

But he does not automatically inhabit every man and woman. We must seek for him earnestly (17), and open the door of our hearts to his knocking (Revelation 3:20).

Prayer

Lord, I thank You that true life and wealth are to be found in the knowledge and love of You.

Keynote

"Seek me early"

Two Invitations

Wisdom (1-6) and **Folly** (13-18) are pictured as two hostesses issuing their invitations, and competing for the patronage of passersby. Outwardly there may appear to be little difference between them, but notice two things: Wisdom offers what she has herself prepared (2), Folly what she has stolen (17); Wisdom rewards her clients with life (6), but Folly with death (18).

Such is still the difference between the offers of Christ and the world. Both seek the souls of men, Christ that he may give them true and lasting wealth, the world that it may delight them with forbidden fruit; Christ that he may reward them with everlasting life, the world that it may lead them into destruction and death.

Verses 7-12 provide further insight. Do you want to know how to tell whether a man is truly wise or foolish? Then courteously correct some fault he has, and see whether he is resentful or grateful (8). If you want another test, offer him some advice (9), and see whether he rejects it or absorbs it. It you want a final test, see whether or not you can detect in him "the fear of the Lord" which "is the beginning of wisdom" (10).

Prayer

Give me Your strength, Lord, to reject every invitation extended to me by the world.

Keynote

"Come...and live" (5-6)

Wisdom for Nations

What makes a country basically happy, prosperous and successful? Is it the possession of great armies, nuclear power, great national resources? It does not say so here. In fact, these verses suggest three quite different things.

● **Political stability** (28). A country whose king, or president, or prime minister, does not enjoy the confidence of the people as a whole is asking for political instability, and is bound to be the prey of coups and revolutions, or else the victim of fear and suppression.

● **Social security** (31). The Lord seems here to be identified with the poor, rather in the same way that Jesus identified himself with the hungry and the sick in Matthew 25:31-46. God's blessing cannot rest upon a country where the poor are exploited and oppressed. Such things must arouse his righteous indignation.

● **Moral integrity** (34). No country has the right to expect prosperity where men and women cannot trust each other implicitly, and where God's laws are not honored and observed. History has often shown that moral decadence has led in the long run to national decline and virtual extinction. God has only pledged himself to honor those who honor him (1 Samuel 2:30).

Prayer

Lord, bless my country and lead it into political, social and moral righteousness.

Keynote

"Righteousness exalts a nation" (34)

Your Introduction to Matthew

What do we know about the writer? Well, we are not *completely* sure that this Gospel was actually written by Matthew, Jesus' tax-collector disciple. But from early times this Gospel was given his name, and it is certainly far more likely than any other suggestion. Of course, he would have used many other people's memories of Jesus as well as his own.

What was the writer aiming at? Like the other three Gospel writers, Matthew aims to give a reliable account of the work and teaching of Jesus Christ. We believe that the Holy Spirit inspired him as he wrote, and we can trust in the accuracy of what we read. Also, as we can tell from all the quotations from the Old Testament, Matthew was particularly anxious to convince the *Jewish* people that Jesus was their true Messiah and King.

What are the special points to watch for? Let's take a clue from chapter 29:19-20, *"Make disciples of all nations...teaching them to observe all that I have commanded you,"* so that men and women shall work together to bring about a new world of peace and justice.

During the next three weeks, we will be meditating on chapters 24-28. This will give us a deep look into Christ's crucifixion and resurrection, the essential events of Jesus' life, and the foundation of our faith and new life in Christ.

God's New Day Dawns

The failure of the Gospel! Do you sometimes feel depressed when you think that after nearly 2,000 years of Christianity the world seems no better than it ever was? Do you feel that somehow the Christian faith has been proved to be a failure? Well, in one sense that's right.

But Christ knew it would be. What did he say there would always be, right up to the day of his return to earth (6-12)? How many different things are mentioned? Have his words come true? So he knew that the Gospel would never capture the hearts of all men. *But we must still do what verse 14 says!*

The triumph of the Gospel! The "failure" isn't the fault of the Gospel itself, which is exactly what men need. Mostly it is that men basically *prefer* to live for themselves. Yet, after men have done their worst, "then the end will come" (14). War, suffering, hatred, treachery, will be over; God's new day will dawn; we shall be with Christ in his Kingdom.

Think ● **What's the use of talking about Jesus Christ if we know that the world is never going to become Christian? How would you answer someone who was discouraged about this?**

Thank God

that he has not cast off this world, but that his Kingdom will surely come.

Keynote

Life up ahead

77

Crisis Days

VERSE
OF THE WEEK
Matthew 25:40

The disciples had asked Jesus two questions: when the Temple would be destroyed (24:2), and what would be the sign of his return to earth (24:3). Matthew runs the two answers into each other. In verses 15-22 Jesus talks about the terrible days that would come in A.D. 70 when the Romans would ruthlessly destroy Jerusalem and massacre its inhabitants. Then he turns to his own coming again. He says it will be:

VERY NECESSARY! The horrors of A.D. 70 have been repeated again and again since then. Hitler's treatment of the Jews was a repeat. Today violence and war and discrimination bring terror into the lives of innocent people. Hold on! Look up! Christ knows, and soon he will come!

VERY SUDDEN! Verse 27 shows that the coming of Christ's Kingdom will not be a *gradual* thing, but instantaneous, and just when people are least expecting it (30).

VERY WELCOME! Verse 31 will really happen! God's children will be delivered in a split second from their anguish, and the crisis will be over!

Think ● **The breakdown of law and order is one sign that Christ's coming is not far off. What should a Christian do in this kind of situation?**

Pray

for Christians in parts of the world where there is much suffering and fear.

Keynote

Holding on and looking up

Don't Be Caught Napping!

Be watchful! Christ isn't one to issue threats. He doesn't say, "Do this, or else...!" But, because of his love for us, he gives us warnings,   such as in today's verses.

We know that his coming will be joyful for us; but it has its solemn aspects, too, for those who have become slack and are caught off guard. We should watch the signs of the times (32-33), things which show that the end of the present age may not be far off.

Be ready! The days of Noah should be a lesson for us. Christ doesn't single out any special sins of the people who died in the flood; *they were simply leading ordinary but thoughtless lives* (38-39). People Christ will leave out of his Kingdom are *folks just doing ordinary jobs* without any special concern about him (40-41). The householder in Christ's story wasn't necessarily doing wrong; he just wasn't ready (43)!

Think ● **What signs do you see that may indicate the nearness of Christ's coming? (Don't exaggerate or invent "signs"!)**

● **Is your life just "ordinary," or is there something special about it for Christ?**

Pray

that Christians everywhere may be ready for Christ's coming by living daringly for him.

Keynote

Today?

Wise and Wicked Leadership

When you come to think of it, most of us have a responsibility for at least one other person. In the light of verses 50 and 51 we would be well advised to check up a little today.

The basic difference between the good and bad leader is that the good one *feeds* his people day by day (45). In a *Christian* sense, this means feeding them on sound truth out of God's Word, the Bible. Isn't it true that many modern ministers will do everything *but* this? The bad leader is one who goes along with the lowest level of morals among his flock, and harms his people rather than helping them to know God better (49). Now some examples:

ARE YOU THE MINISTER OF A CHURCH? You must try to be as up-to-date and "with it" as you can. But how faithfully are you carrying out your *first* responsibility?

ARE YOU THE LEADER OF A GROUP? Every church group should have as a primary aim bringing God's word to the members.

ARE YOU THE HEAD OF A FAMILY? I hope that Jesus, when he comes, will find you "so doing" (46)!

Think ● **Would the same words of Christ apply to people who *ought* to be taking on responsibility but are refusing to do so?**

Pray

for the minister, leaders and parents in your own church.

Keynote

"So doing"

Lamps But No Oil

This is a simple story, but the meaning is important. It's more about the *foolish* girls than about the *wise* ones, so let's see what the Lord Jesus was getting at.

They were with all the others, waiting for the Bridegroom. The "Bridegroom" stands for Christ, and all ten girls said they were waiting for him to come. So the five foolish ones stand for members of churches who profess to be good Christians along with everyone else.

They had lamps like the rest. No doubt they were all dressed properly for the occasion. *So far as you could see,* everything was fine. But *what you couldn't see* was that it was just outward show, with nothing inside to make it genuine!

They had no oil. In spite of all appearances, they weren't ready. And when the Bridegroom came, it was too late. Before they could put matters right, the door was finally and permanently *shut.* There was no "second chance."

Think ● **Are you SURE that Christ "knows you" (12) and that you are INWARDLY ready to meet him?**

Pray

for a true faith in Jesus Christ, and that your heart may be given to him.

Keynote

Time is running out

Hope for the One-Talent Man

Today's Note is for those who think they have only "one talent" compared with the many gifts other Christians have. This one-talent man, by his foolishness, lost all his chances.

What he had. One talent. Perhaps you think *you* don't have any talents at all? No! EVERYBODY HAS AT LEAST ONE. If you have Christ in your heart, you have an ability to love, and there are ways for you to express that love, if you want to.

What he felt. Well, what does the man with one talent usually feel? I think he often *resents* the fact that he's been given less than others. He feels bitter, and ashamed at not being able to keep up with the rest. He may feel jealous, too. THE PERSON WITH ONE TALENT IS MORE LIKELY TO FAIL HIS LORD THAN THE PERSON WITH FIVE! He's so busy wishing he had more to work with, that he doesn't use what he has.

What he missed. Compare verses 21 and 23. See any differences? No, there aren't any. The rewards for the five-talent and two-talent men were identical, and it would have been the same for the third man, too. THERE IS AS MUCH JOY IN USING ONE TALENT WELL AS IN USING FIVE!

Think ● about verse 29. Use what talent you have, and it will grow. Neglect it, and you'll have nothing.

Pray

for God's help in making your love available to the world.

Keynote

Use it or lose it

Sheep and Goats

Look at Jesus Christ. "Son of man" was his name while on earth the first time, to express his lowliness and oneness with us. How differently the name will sound the *next* time he comes (31)! We will see Jesus as King of all the nations (34). If we serve him, we aren't serving a nobody, but the King of men and angels.

Look at yourself. If there is one lesson in this story, it is that *words* without *actions* reveal a heart that is all wrong. Everyone called Jesus "Lord" (37,44). Nothing necessarily wrong with their beliefs or their words, was there? But the ones on the left hand had never put into practice any belief which they might have held, and had never realized that failure to act with the love of Christ was equal to turning one's back on him (44). What made the "righteous" ones different was that their hearts were so full of Christ's love that they instantly saw a brother in need (whatever his appearance or his merits or demerits) and did something about it.

Think ● **Have you recently done any of the things in verses 35 and 36?** *If not, why not?* **Don't rush around making up for it; check the state of your heart first.**

Pray

that Christians may not be unpleasant "do-gooders," but may serve the needy out of a heart-felt love for people.

Keynote

"You did it to me"

Sat. 10th week MATTHEW 26:1-13

Impulse Versus Logic

You can divide people roughly into those who are IMPULSIVE and those who are LOGICAL. I wonder which you come under! Today notice how both LOGIC and IMPULSE are important.

Some people need to be more logical. Take those "chief priests," for instance (3-5). They were following IMPULSES, but the IMPULSES were leading them to evil. They needed to use more LOGIC, and say to themselves, "This Man Jesus is just the kind of person the Bible says God will send; he's doing just the right kind of works and giving the right kind of teaching. Maybe we'd better give him a hearing." Yes, you have been given a brain. Use it, even if you are the impulsive type!

Some people need to be more impulsive. Those disciples were obviously good at managing money, and became upset when they saw what the woman was doing (8). LOGICALLY they were absolutely right in what they said (9), but Jesus cast *his* vote for the woman's IMPULSE. You see, when impulse is tamed by God's Spirit, it can produce some "beautiful things" (10).

Think ● Weren't the disciples just saying what Jesus himself had said in 25:35-36? How would you answer that one?

Pray *for more logic or more impulse, whichever you think you need.*

Keynote The heart has its reasons

84

Depends How You Use It

Money — curse or blessing? Well, here are examples of both.

Money misused (14-16 and 20-25). Some people try to make Judas seem a more noble character than he really was. They suggest, for example, that he felt Jesus was being too slow to declare himself, and that the "betrayal" would force him to take the plunge and make himself King. But if you stick to the story in the Bible, I'm afraid you can't escape the conclusion that Judas simply reached the point where *money was more important to him than Christ was.*

Money well-used (17-19). Jesus had several friends who were quite well off. He didn't criticize them or tell them to get rid of their money. For instance, the man (18) who lent Jesus the large upstairs room for the Last Supper must have had a big house and been quite rich. The difference between him and Judas is that *all the man possessed was dedicated to Jesus* and ready for him to use. On *those* terms, it is not a sin to be rich.

Think ● **In what ways today may followers of Jesus betray him for money? Think of more ways of using what *you* have for Christ: your money, your home, your time.**

Pray

that Christians everywhere may use their possessions for Christ and for those he died to save.

Keynote

"Is it I, Lord?"

A Matter of Life and Death

When you next come to the communion service, keep two thoughts in mind about it, both connected with death.

It spells death for Christ. The broken bread and the poured-out wine can mean only one thing: the flesh and blood of Jesus handed over to death because of us. We all had a share in his crucifixion; each one of us had a hand on the hammer that drove in the nails. That's *our* contribution to the cross!

It spells death to our pride. Not much to be proud of, is it? And each time we hold the bread and take the cup we remember that if there is *anything* in us of any value to God, it is zero per cent ourselves (not even one per cent) and 100 per cent Christ. So what is the point of boasting about ourselves?

Peter hadn't understood any of this. "Though they all fall away because of you, *I* will never fall away!" he said. It sounded grand, but actually it was the opposite of what he *should* have said. His independence and pride came bubbling to the top. He would have to learn his lesson the hard way.

Think ● After Christ's words in verse 31, what *should* Peter have said?

Pray

that from yourself you may expect nothing, but that from Christ you may expect everything.

Keynote

"Beneath the cross of Jesus..."

Companions in Gethsemane

Where does Gethsemane fit into the scheme of things? Here is one explanation.

You cannot *serve* the world in the best way until you have first *wept over it*. It is a mistake many of us make. Out of a "do-good" mentality we can get involved in all kinds of community affairs and evangelistic ventures, but there is no *heart* in it all. When that is the case, the world doesn't need this kind of service.

Christ was "sorrowful and troubled" (37). He agonized over the world with all its evil, and over the painful work he had to do. He secluded himself and wept and prayed and pleaded. Then he was ready to tackle what had to be done.

He needed companions in his agony. These were supposed to be Peter, James and John, but they failed. He needs companions to share his agony today, too; Christians who will look at the people who have cheated them, the politicians who don't care if their people starve, the empty wasteland of television, the junkies living through the horrors of drugs, the destruction of moral standards one by one, and just *grieve before God.* Then when Christ says, "Rise, let us be going" (46), their actions will spring from a deeply loving heart.

Think ● What may this kind of experience do for you (39)?

Pray

that we may not fail Christ in his agony, or the world in its need.

Keynote

"Watch with me" (38)

"With Swords and Clubs"

That's *one* way of tackling a situation! As a matter of fact, people tried to deal with matters that night in at least three different ways.

How Judas saw the situation. Judas had made a fateful decision — to give up his grasp of Christ and look after "number one." Already we see him sinking lower: using a greeting and a kiss as a signal to Christ's enemies. There will be no way back: Judas slowly sinks into despair.

How the disciples saw the situation. Their answer to it was to protest, to demonstrate, to resort to violence. They tried to force circumstances to do what *they* wanted, and when they found it couldn't be done, their bravado collapsed and they deserted Jesus (56). Despair again.

How Christ saw the situation. Twice he gave us the clue to his attitude (54,56). He found the meaning of his own life in the Scriptures, not in circumstances or in his own ideas. So he relaxed and let things go their way. He knew you can only conquer evil with good.

Think ● **Is it *always* right to let events take their course without doing anything to change them? Why was it right *this* time?**

Pray

that you may not fight against things that are God's will, but always win over them by patience and the quality of your life.

Keynote

"Overcome evil with good"

The Priests and the Prisoner

Though the priests didn't realize it, *they* were the ones on trial — everyone is, when he faces Jesus Christ! Compare the priests and the Prisoner, and reach your verdict.

The priests. First, note *they had already made up their minds before hearing the evidence* (59). That's not as rare as you might think; if you watch carefully, you'll find that few days pass without your doing it at least once. But it is serious, as you realize when people do it to you! Note also *their obvious relish of the chance to humiliate* Jesus and cause him distress. Sometimes it is necessary to criticize someone; but do it with genuine love, not malice.

The Prisoner. The important thing is that *he didn't stoop to the methods of his enemies* (63). Think of our own day. Men and women, in the name of civil liberty or peace or justice, have hurled abuse, stirred up violence, thrown bombs. But others have achieved *more* by their dignity and their willingness to suffer for their faith. They stand with Christ.

Think • **After keeping quiet so long, why did Christ say what he did in verse 64?**

Pray *that in all of life's situations you may know when to be quiet, when to speak, and what to say.*

Keynote **When silence is golden**

To Fall –and Rise Again

The way down. If you feel you are prone to let your Lord down, take heart from this story about a leader among the apostles. Asked if he belonged to Christ, Peter took three downward steps:

"He denied it" (70). Perhaps he didn't want to embarrass the company. You recognize the kind of situation? The kind of place where you feel it would be out of place to talk about Christ. *But it isn't!*

"He denied it with an oath" (72). By this time Peter can see he's getting in deep. His oath was in hope they would now leave him alone. But it was wrong; he should have owned up to his first lie and set the record straight.

"He began to invoke a curse on himself" (74). Now he is in an agony of fear and self-disgust. He's down as far as he can go.

The way back up. *"Peter remembered the saying of Jesus"* (75). To remember words of Jesus that we have perhaps deliberately been forgetting is a start. "He wept bitterly." Grief that one has wandered far from God is not a curse but one of the Christian's greatest blessings. It carries you a long way back.

Think ● This story shows Peter in a bad light. Why did God want it put in the Bible?

Pray

that God will help you never to take that first step out of his will.

Keynote

The end of self-confidence

Conscience

The horror of having a conscience. Judas thought he could forget the example Christ had set him, and live just for himself. But — *You can't escape conscience forever.* "When Judas saw Jesus condemned..." (3), the sword went through his heart. *You can't come back whenever you want.* "He repented" (3). Truly? The New English Bible has what seems to be a better translation, "He was seized with *remorse.*" Repentance is a blessing, but remorse is a nightmare. *You can't turn the clock back.* "He brought back the thirty pieces of silver" (3). Sorry, Judas, what's done is done. You must live with it (4) or *die* with it (5).

The horror of not having a conscience. There is a sense in which those priests were even more horrifying than Judas was. What cynicism! Presumably that money came *out* of the Temple treasury to be paid to Judas, but now it can't be put *back* because it's "blood money" (6). They'll stick to some phony religious law, but when a man comes to them in distress, these shepherds of God's flock say, "What do *we* care? That's *your* problem!" (4). Judas can go to hell — they could not care less!

Think ● **Is it ever right to go against your conscience? Is it ever right to suppress it?**

Pray

that your conscience may always be your friend, not your enemy.

Keynote

Dead end

Barabbas or Christ

**VERSE
OF THE WEEK
Matthew 28:19**

We still have to choose between Barabbas and Christ.

Barabbas. He was a bandit (John 18:40, NEB), an outlaw, perhaps looked upon as a kind of Jewish Robin Hood! He fought against the Romans, not against his own people. He was a revolutionary and a murderer (Mark 15:7), and was in jail.

He stands for some things that are popular today. He was for *nationalism* — the demand of each minority group to withdraw unto itself and manage its own affairs; for *a hard line* — his sworn hatred of Rome would be popular; and for *violent action* — a program which is easier to sell than wiser but slower methods. Who stands for "Barabbas" in your own country?

Christ. Compared with Barabbas, Christ seems much less attractive; he looks colorless, weak, soft. He wasn't a nationalist, he wouldn't condemn Rome, and he refused to tell people to fight. He was just pure goodness. He wouldn't even argue or defend himself (12-14). But when it comes to the crux of the matter, the biggest question in your life is not, "What shall I do with Barabbas?" but, "What shall I do with Jesus?" (22).

Think ● Why did Jesus refuse to answer? Are you good at keeping quiet when necessary?

Pray

for the patience of Jesus, plus his humility and his dignity.

Keynote

The biggest choice in history

Guilty or Not Guilty?

Two men here aren't what they seem.

The "innocent" one who was really guilty (24-26). He said, "I am innocent of this man's blood" (24). But he said it himself; nobody else did and I'm sure it wasn't *God's* opinion. He "washed his hands" but the guilt lay on his heart. Jesus was innocent; Pilate knew quite well what he should do. James 4:17 says, "If anyone knows a good thing he should do, and does not do it, that is a sin for him." He was afraid that to let Jesus go would start a riot; he thought that to let the people have their way would be safer. But he should have done what was *right* whatever the cost.

The "guilty" One who was really innocent (27-31). Here's the greatest example of One who refused to "wash his hands" of those who need him, whatever it cost him. He gave himself to torture, shame and death for them. *Christ confronts you today* in the war orphan, the crippled child, the millions who have never heard the Gospel, the poverty-stricken, the cancer patient — someone who needs your love on your own street or in your own house.

Think ● What "good thing" do you know you should do? Are you guilty or innocent?

Pray

that your heart will never rest until you've paid your debt.

Keynote

"If anyone knows a good thing he should do..."

The Last Agony

These hours at Golgotha are the climax of all Christ came to do. See how he tackled them.

His weakness. A prisoner always carried his own cross to the place of execution. What happened in verse 32 shows that Christ had collapsed through weakness. He had to face his great ordeal when he was physically least capable of doing so, but he kept going. God may lead you to a similar experience.

His determination. The drink offered in verse 34 was intended to dull pain; but it blurred the mind, and Christ was determined to keep his full faculties at this crucial time. He had to see it through to the end; I think *we* often try to escape from unpleasant situations.

His endurance. Just glance at verses 39 to 44 again, and try to picture what this abuse must have meant to Christ. Then picture it going on for three hours, from 9 a.m. ("the third hour," Mark 15:25) to 12 noon ("the sixth hour," Matthew 27:45). How much can you take?

Think ● **Read what the priests said in the first sentence of verse 42. In what sense were they right and in what sense wrong? The fact that he *could* have saved himself made his sacrifice even greater!**

Pray

that your devotion to Christ may be worthy of his devotion to you.

Keynote

Held to the cross by love

Uttermost Love

"The greatest love a man can have for his friends is to give his life for them" (John 15:13, TEV). Christ perfectly fulfilled his own saying.

The meaning of it — for Christ. We get a glimpse of what this meant for Christ in verse 46. In that time of "darkness" (45) all the hellish nightmare of all the evil in creation was laid upon Jesus, as he brought his pure body to the sacrifice. Even his Father turned his back in the moment. *"We may not know, we cannot tell, what pains he had to bear."*

The meaning of it — for mankind. Verse 51 was a visual aid. The curtain, or veil, in the Temple, kept people away from the actual presence of God. It was ripped apart from the *top* —from *God* — to show that *through Jesus* the way to God is open again. Our wickedness, which kept us at arm's length, had been paid for.

The meaning of it — for me. I stand with the centurion (54). I see Christ die. I am filled with awe. I bow my head and heart and confess Jesus as Son of God. *I am never the same again.*

Think ● **Christ's sufferings were great because my sin was great. The way I serve men in Christ's name should be just as great, too.**

Pray

that all who have never heard may know of Jesus' love for them.

Keynote

He gave his life that I might give mine

"Make It as Secure as You Can!"

What did Pilate mean by these words? Was he being sarcastic, or did he have an idea in the back of his mind just how futile the Jews' efforts were? Whatever the answer, things couldn't have been more difficult for any kind of *faked* "resurrection." There was:

A SHROUD (59). This was a long winding-sheet; Jesus was bound hand and foot.

A STONE (60). As with Daniel in the lions' den, Jesus was locked in by a great stone and left for dead. No chance of his reviving and slipping out unseen.

A SEAL (66). On the outside of the tomb an official seal impression was affixed, so that the stone could not be moved without breaking the seal. This was done in cases where extreme security was essential.

A SENTRY (66). In fact, as we learn from 28:4, more than one. The chief priests were really anxious, and, as it turned out, they were quite right to be. In spite of all the precautions, God was planning to have the last word.

Think ● Some people are just as anxious today not to have Jesus running loose. How do they try to hem him in and tie him down?

Pray *that the mighty, risen Christ may be let loose on the whole world.*

Keynote **Man cannot make the chain that God cannot break**

"Risen, As He Said!"

What a difference it makes to death! The shroud, the stone, the seal, the sentries — all speak of death: final, unbeatable death. A touch of God's finger, and the sentries fall back, the seal is broken, the stone rolls away, the shroud is left behind — *Christ is risen!*

Vainly they watch his bed —
Jesus, my Savior!
Vainly they seal the dead —
Jesus, my Lord!

Now the graveyard is an "intermediate stop," not the "end of the line."

What a difference it makes to life! To try to do any good in this world without Christ is a thankless task. You meet constant failure all the way, because of human nature, because of death, because of your own frailty. But the resurrection of Jesus means not just the end of Death (capital "D") but the beginning of Life (capital "L"). You can tackle your world — *and change it* — in Christ's strength.

Think ● Despondent, dispirited Christian living is a denial of Christ's resurrection. In what ways do you expect Christ's risen power to affect your life this week?

Pray

for all who mourn, that God will lift their eyes and hearts.

Keynote

"Come, see! — Go, tell!" (6,10)

A Story to Tell

The guards have a story to tell (11-15). You can hardly believe it. The guards actually saw the resurrection take place; they run to the chief priests with the news. Now the priests know that Jesus was what he claimed to be — the Son of God. But instead of acting on it, they give the guards a story to tell that is a fantastic mixture of lies and deceit. And this is what so many have done with the Gospel ever since. If it weren't so, we might long ago have had a world with no war, no hunger, no poverty, no hatred. God's verdict is in John 3:19, "Light has come into the world, but *men have preferred darkness to light,* because they do evil."

The disciples have a story to tell (16-20).No matter if some people won't accept it — *our job is to tell the good news!* Note what we must aim for (19-20):

TO MAKE DISCIPLES — to bring people to a clear step of conversion to Christ.

TO BAPTIZE — to build them into a living fellowship of committed persons.

TO TEACH — to get them to live in their society the kind of all-out life that Christ commanded.

Think ● Test your aims in life by those three commands of Christ.

Pray

that you may fulfill your part in Christ's great plan for the world.

Keynote

Christ has power (18) and you have Christ (20)

Your Introduction to Exodus

The second book in the Bible carries the story of God's dealings with men an important stage farther than **Genesis,** the first book. The descendants of Abraham, with whom God had made his covenant, were slaves in Egypt. From their ranks God preserved, prepared and called Moses to give them liberty. They were redeemed by a demonstration of the power of God that was to be commemorated by the annual observance of Passover.

To some extent welded into a community, Israel as a nation was brought into covenant relationship with Jehovah. He pledged himself to be their God and to care for them, while they in their turn undertook to love and obey him. Detailed instructions were given them regarding their religious life as well as their ethical duties.

Christians can hardly fail to read *Exodus* in the light of the redemption that Christ has secured for them from the power of sin and Satan. They too constitute a special community, the people of God, who stand in covenant relationship with him. But while this relationship carries with it moral and religious obligations, it is guaranteed by the fact of their union with Christ their Redeemer, through saving faith.

Our Notes will cover chapters 1-14, the background and exciting events of God's deliverance of the Israelites from Egypt.

Toughening Up

**VERSE
OF THE WEEK
Exodus 4:12**

Confronted by a bunch of raw recruits, the sergeant shouts, "I'll soon make men out of you!" He takes them out on the assault course, and makes them go through all kinds of hardships in all kinds of weather. It's not long before they are tough enough to face anything.

Often God handles his sons and daughters in the same way. For instance, the "sons of Israel" in Egypt needed to be trained for the work God had for them to do. So —

● **Rigor.** God knew what was happening when the Egyptians "made the people of Israel serve with rigor" (13), or "treated their Israelite slaves with ruthless severity" (NEB). He hadn't forgotten them. Nor has he forgotten *us* when he allows hard times to come and our lives are made "bitter" (14). It's the toughening-up process, leading to —

● **Vigor.** No doubt about the connection (12)! The one led to the other. The harder the times they had to go through, the tougher they became and the more vigorously they grew in numbers. The same is often true of the church, as well.

Think ● God has promised that you will never be tested beyond your ability to bear it (1 Corinthians 10:13). Then what should be your attitude to hardships?

Pray

that you may see God's purpose behind every testing that comes to you.

Keynote

Let every rigor lead to vigor

The Age-Old "Race Problem"

The "race problem" wasn't invented in the 20th century, for it existed over 3,000 years ago. Pharaoh was faced by a vigorous racial minority, and he tackled it in typical fashion.

● **The way of fear.** You can sense Pharaoh's *fear* of the Israelites in verses 9 and 10. As a result, he started on a policy of repression. He couldn't picture his nation consisting of people of various races and beliefs, all living together in equality. So he oppressed the people who were different from himself. When his idea in verse 11 didn't work, he tried a new tack (16).

This behavior is always a sign of fear and insecurity. There are much better ways to solve the problem.

● **The way of courage.** The Hebrew wives acted with great bravery. Their situation was as dangerous as any under Hitler in World War II, yet they weren't afraid. Why not? See verse 17. If you "fear" God (honor and serve him), you needn't be afraid of anyone or anything. As the old Scottish hymn says:

Fear him, ye saints, and you will then
Have nothing else to fear!

Think ● **What is the connection between fear and hatred?**

Pray

for Christ to work wherever in the world there is fear and violence.

Keynote

They served a greater King

God Takes a Hand

It would be wrong to imagine that God doesn't watch over the kind of unjust situation we read about yesterday. Sooner or later his justice will catch up with men who cruelly dominate other people. The same is true today, whether it's a matter of harsh management, racial injustice, or any other form of oppression. God will put matters right.

● **God's timing is exact.** Exact to *him,* though *to us* it often seems terribly slow. In today's verses we are reading about the birth of Moses; he will be 80 years old by the time he leads the Israelites out of Egypt. So almost all the men who have suffered in chapter 1 will be dead before God sets the people free. We get so impatient with God; we think that if he doesn't do something RIGHT NOW it will be too late. We needn't worry, he has things in hand.

● **God's planning is perfect.** This passage is full of "coincidences." You don't really think they are coincidences, do you? No, they are God's perfect planning — all worked out so that Moses will grow up with his own people, yet have the benefit of the finest Egyptian education and upbringing.

Think ● As you look back at your life, can you see the many ways in which God has worked all things together?

Pray

that God will prepare the younger generation to be his agents.

Keynote

In his own way

It's Nearly Time

Most of us find it very hard to wait. Especially if time is slipping away and problems are getting worse. This was the experience of the Israelites in Egypt — they were impatient and discouraged. But unknown to them, the time was ripening for their deliverance.

● **Moses is almost ready.** If he had tried to lead the people at the age of 40, he would perhaps have made dreadful mistakes and the result would have been disastrous for them all. He had much to learn in handling people and situations (11-15). But there followed 40 years' experience of life, especially in the desert through which he would have to lead the people (15-22).

● **Israel is almost ready.** For many years they had been suffering, and their lives had been bitter. Now another element is added — it's in verse 23. They learned to do one vital thing which made them ready for God's help.

● **God is almost ready.** In verses 24-25 there are four things we can learn about God. He didn't take *action* yet, but these four things made him ready to do so. The time is near for him to take the lead.

Think ● **Are you impatient with God? Are you becoming upset because you want him to act faster than he's prepared to?**

       ● **Are you getting ready for Christ's service by learning more about life and God?**

Pray   for God's purposes to be worked out in your life.

Keynote   **In training**

Marching Orders

Moses received something we all need — a call from God that suddenly made sense and gave him *something to live for*. For a long time he had been living the nomadic, desert life, looking after sheep; but a sudden and strange event gave him a fixed compass bearing. There were three parts to this great experience:

● **A good view of God.** Moses saw a blazing bush that showed him how pure and powerful God is. From that time on, God was Someone he'd *met*. From verses 7-12 you could make a list of at least eight things God showed Moses about himself.

● **A good view of himself.** Here's a test for you: what difference do you see between Moses in verse 11 and Moses in chapter 2 verse 12? Has his attitude changed? Did God's words in verse 5 make some difference?

● **A good view of his work.** Once you've had a clear vision of God and of yourself, you're ready to be shown what God has for you to do. Moses wasn't shown *all* of it — just the next step (10).

Think ● *Where* people met God: MOSES — in his daily work. ISAIAH — praying in the Temple. EZEKIEL — thinking by a river. PAUL — on a journey. Do you think God still meets people like this today? Can he meet you this way?

Prayer

for a clear call from God, the wisdom to recognize it, and the strength to obey it.

Keynote

Direction

The God We Adore

In the conversation Moses had with God in today's verses is the foundation for the great work that Moses did during the rest of his life. *He really got a grasp of the kind of God he was serving.*

● **God's personality.** Look at the name he learned for God, *"I am who I am"* (14).

It's a name that tells us a great deal. The original words include the idea, "I was who I was," and, "I will be who I will be." So God has no beginning or end. He calls himself "I am," so he needs no help or advice; he's complete and perfect and magnificent. *It's a name that hides a great deal.* It's a mysterious kind of name, that leaves us wondering. His name is a reminder that we will never find out everything about God, not even all we'd like to.

● **God's purpose.** God doesn't withdraw somewhere a few million miles away, and ponder his own greatness. He lives here, for us, just as he expects us to live for him. All his knowledge and his power are put to work on behalf of the people who love him, as you'll know if you study verses 17,20-21. This is "the God we adore"!

Think ● **Do you feel we sometimes get too familiar with God?**

Worship

God in his greatness and thank *him for his love.*

Keynote

God forever, God for all

Trust God and Go Ahead

● **People are amazingly slow to believe.** God saw that Moses, in spite of the blazing bush, and the great name of God he had learned, still only saw his own weakness (1)! Humility is a Christian virtue, *but there is a point where humility turns into an escape,* and becomes either the sin of laziness, or the sin of unbelief in God.

● **God is amazingly slow to give up.** Instead of criticizing Moses for his objections, God does everything to help him, and the Israelites believe. He even produces three miracles (2-9).

But still Moses said, "Oh, Lord, send someone else!" (13). And finally God got angry (14). Why was Moses in the wrong?

He had a clear call from God. God never asks us to do anything we cannot do — with his strength. If you believe God is calling you to something you feel is beyond you — some new responsibility, leadership, or speaking out — *go ahead!*

He had a clear promise from God (12). The promises came true. After the first few times, Moses hardly ever needed Aaron's help. Read God's promises in the Bible, believe them, swallow hard, then *go ahead!*

Think ● **Is any of your potential as a Christian being wasted because you lack the courage to use it?**

Pray

that you may be alert to see where God is leading you, and quick to follow.

Keynote

Impossible? Try it anyway.

Hindrance and Help

VERSE
OF THE WEEK
Exodus 6:7

● **Moses and his wife (24-26).** To understand this situation, we have to try to read between the lines. Moses had done what many, even in ancient times, seemed to do: he had made an unwise marriage. His wife was a Midianite girl, probably not a believer in Moses' God. Apparently she had objected to God's command that male children should be circumcised, and Moses had gone along with her. But *this had to be set right before Moses could be used to pass on God's Word to others.* So God used a severe illness to bring Moses to the point of obedience (24), and (still protesting) Zipporah cooperated.

Many today are trying to live their Christian faith in the midst of opposition from husband or wife. *It affects our service for God,* and drains us of energy. *It affects our children,* and tends to keep them from God (circumcision was a mark of belonging to the Lord). It's a situation to be prayed over, and put right.

● **Moses and his brother** (27-31). How different! Aaron was a man with his ear open to God (27), ready to play a role subordinate to his younger brother Moses (30), bringing faith and happiness into other lives (31).

Think ● **The family that works together for Christ experiences a special unity and love.**

Pray

that you may encourage rather than hinder others in serving God.

Keynote

Partnership

Disappointment

- **Picture the scene.** Hopes are running high (4:31). After praying and worshiping God, the Israelite people watch Moses and Aaron go off to see Pharaoh. At last the great day has come when they are going to be set free!

- **Then the shock.** Moses and Aaron come back with solemn faces. "Pharaoh turned us down," they say. "He says he doesn't know our God and we must all get back to work."

- **Then worse news still.** The Egyptian slavedrivers tell them that new regulations have been made which will mean much harder work on the part of every one of them. They will be treated without mercy.

- **And so the people sink** into one of the worst periods in their lives. Disappointment afflicts them until they are all but crushed. Their faith in their God is tried to the breaking point.

Yet the important point is that *God was never nearer to them.* He had foreseen exactly what Pharaoh would say and do (3:19), and had his plans all made.

Think ● **Sometimes we're so close to the *detail* of what is happening that it's hard to see God's over-all plan. Is this your experience?**

Pray

that your faith may not break down in the tough spots of life.

Keynote

Darkest hour before dawn

Leadership Crisis

Almost immediately Moses finds himself in a difficult position! He's hardly been accepted by the people as their chief when he faces a major crisis. His whole leadership hangs in the balance.

● **The people blame Moses!** That's how it often is. It is hard for the rank and file to take setbacks; they quickly lose heart and then find someone to blame (20-21).

Moses blamed the Lord!

(a) He questioned God's GOODNESS (22).

(b) He questioned God's CALL (22).

(c) He questioned God's ABILITY (23).

The leader must always be much tougher than the people he leads. One of the chief marks of leadership is to keep calm and keep thinking when others are losing their heads, and to keep in touch with the Lord when others are turning away. Of course, Moses was right to go to the Lord, but not in a spirit of *complaint.*

Think ● **"The leader must always be much tougher than the people." How can he be?**

Pray *for the qualities of leadership needed in the work to which God has called you.*

Keynote **Hold on!**

Free-to Serve God

Although you may never have had the experience of being set free from slavery like the Israelites, there is a very real parallel between what God did for them and what God does for us.

● **God sees our helpless condition.** Nothing escapes him (5). He sees our bondage (to sin, to habits, to a way of life): He hears our groaning (at our sufferings, our fears). He loves us; he has pity on us.

● **God acts for our deliverance.** Moses couldn't do a thing; but *God* could — and did! Look at verse 6. *This is what God did in Jesus Christ on the cross.* He got us out from under our old life of guilt and impotence; he freed us from it with arms outstretched and with a mighty act of love.

● **God makes us his people.** This is our new status as believers in Christ (7). There's a new sense of *belonging* — we belong to the Lord and the Lord to us.

And the new land which God promised to the Israelites (8)? That can be likened to the new life, the new purpose in living, the new hope, that the Lord has given us.

Think ● **Are there people who stay away from Christ for the same reasons given in verse 9?**

Pray

for all whose life is a burden, that they may find release in Christ.

Keynote

God of the open door

One's Just Desserts

"I will assert my power in Egypt..." (4,NEB). Great events were taking place in those days, as they are today. History was being written. A nation was being born; another nation was to suffer the results of fighting against God. But it wasn't just happening by chance; *God* was the One who was handing out prosperity to one and punishment to the other.

The Bible teaches that God judges *nations* as well as *individuals.* Nations reap the fruit of their own deeds and policies. It's clear enough here:

● **Egypt was ripe for God's judgment.** Pharaoh headed a vicious, cruel regime, and refused to listen to reason or to appeals (4,13). *Result:* "Great acts of judgment" (4).

● **Israel was ripe for God's help.** Moses, for all his questions and excuses, really did want to serve God, as you can see from his obedience in verses 6 and 10. And although the people's faith wavered, they were surely on God's side. *Result:* "I will bring my people out" (4).

Think ● **Where do you think your own nation stands today, so far as God is concerned?**

● **Check on your own life from this point of view.**

Pray

for your country, its people, its leaders, and its influence.

Keynote

"What a man sows..."

The Lord my Enemy

God never does anything without a good reason. He wasn't inflicting these troubles on the Egyptians just to "show off"; he wasn't even "twisting Pharaoh's arm," so that he would let the Israelites go. No, every one of the "plagues of Egypt" tied in with Pharaoh's hostile and obstinate state of heart.

● **God opposed Pharaoh's idols.** The plagues were to show the Egyptians that their so-called gods were no gods at all. One of the most sacred objects in Egypt was the River Nile, and it is struck in the very first plague. If Pharaoh had an eye for the facts, he should have seen he was fighting against the true God.

● **God opposed Pharaoh's pride.** Pharaoh was obsessed with his own might. God wanted him to see himself as he really was. It was a big undertaking, but see where God starts. The Nile was the very lifeblood of Egypt (and still is); without it Egypt would be a dead land. God touches it through Moses' rod, and produces a major crisis for Egypt.

When God deals with us severely, he's not just toying with us. He wants to expose our false "gods" for what they are; he wants to break our harmful pride.

Think ● Does this mean that God's judgments are an expression of love?

Pray

that you may never force the Lord to become your enemy.

Keynote

You can't hold out against God

Getting the Point Across

God is communicating with Pharaoh in a way he should be able to understand, but it's not leading to any results. One wonders whether the world rulers today are any wiser when it comes to recognizing and following the "signs of the times."

● **God's persuasion.** Once again, God struck at the false Egyptian religion, for the frog was a sacred creature, and the symbol of one of their chief gods. Surely they would learn their lesson now? Also, it's worth mentioning that *they weren't allowed to kill a frog;* so just imagine how unpleasant it must have been to have them swarming around *without being able to do anything about them!* It should have been enough to stir up public opinion!

● **God's mercy.** "Some mercy!" you may say. But these first few plagues were fairly insignificant compared with those to come; if only Pharaoh and his people had taken the hint, nothing worse need have happened. In the first plague, God left a way for the people to get pure water (7:24); while the frogs were no worse than unpleasant.

Think ● **In what ways may God today give gentle warnings when we are out of his way for us? What may be the consequences of ignoring them?**

Pray

that the churches today may understand what God is saying to them.

Keynote

Distant early warning

The Campaign Intensifies

VERSE
OF THE WEEK
Exodus 9:14

● **The plagues get more destructive.** God is very gradually making the plagues *more serious.* *The effect* begins to hurt. The insects attacked the bodies of the people and their animals (18).

The magicians, able up to now to copy each plague, bowed out of the contest (19).

The Israelites from now on were protected from the plagues.

● **The Pharaoh gets more desperate.** Pharaoh's reactions are getting desperate, and we can see in the mistakes he made the pattern followed by nations and individuals today.

In times of difficulty, they put God off. He puts off submitting to God until the last possible moment.

In times of crisis, they cry to God. When they've exhausted every human possibility, they turn to God in prayer (28).

In times of relief, they forget God. God, in his kindness, answered those prayers (31). Crisis over, they're right back to the old ways again (32).

Think ● **Have you prayed intensely to God, and made promises to him that you haven't kept?**

Pray

for forgiveness if this is so, and for help in putting it right.

Keynote

Don't be a crisis Christian

A Turning Point

This is a terrible turning point in the story. Here's why.

● **Another "first":** the first recorded deaths due to the plagues (6). But, because of God's mercy, *it was cattle that died!* A clear warning of what was to come, but it was ignored.

● **Another "first":** the first disease caused to humans (11). But because of God's mercy, *it was not a fatal one!* But it does seem to have been a very unpleasant and painful one, and again it should have been a clear enough warning to Pharaoh not to trifle with God any longer.

● **Another "first":** the most serious one of all; it's in verse 12. For the first time since the plagues have started, we read that *the Lord himself* makes Pharaoh's heart hard and obstinate. What can this mean? Simply that if you set your heart often enough against God, he will agree with your decision, and leave you to form even more bitterness and hostility. In the end, it becomes so hard for you to change your mind as to be virtually impossible.

Think ● **Every time we disobey some word of God to us, or just ignore it, it becomes harder to hear and obey the next time. If you've been closing your ears to something God is saying, change your mind today!**

Pray

for a quick response each time God gives you his directions.

Keynote

"He did not listen" (12)

Injustice Doesn't Pay

● **It was a question of simple justice.** The Israelites were being held as slaves and forced to labor. Even by the standards of those days there was no justification for this. They were not criminals, not even prisoners of war. They had come voluntarily to Egypt and been invited by a previous Pharaoh to settle (Genesis 47:5-6). The economy had now become dependent on this free labor, and it was hard for Pharaoh to set them free; *but a nation must do what is right, not merely follow its own interests.* Pray that your nation may always act justly.

● **It was a question of simple obstinacy.** Pharaoh must have seen that what God said in verse 15 was right (RSV); he owed his very life to God's patience. So do many nations, and many people today. If God stepped in, they'd vanish in a puff of smoke. Yet, in spite of God's gentleness with them, they will not turn to him. It's plain obstinacy. But God will make things tougher and tougher for them, as he did for Pharaoh and the Egyptians.

Think ● **Today all kinds of social groups are motivated by their own interests, rather than by a sense of justice for all — for example: employers, unions, students — yes, even churches themselves. What can you do to help promote justice?**

Pray

for a greater spirit of brotherhood among people of all kinds.

Keynote

"Still exalting yourself" (17)

Living for the Moment

Here's a man who lives by impulse, not by principle. He has many imitators today!

● **"Sin when it seems natural!"** Pharaoh thought he could get away with it, so he left the Jews enslaved. That seems to be the only question asked, "Can I get away with it!" It's dangerous when your attitude to what you know to be wrong is governed by whether it's likely to be found out.

● **"Ignore God when it is convenient!"** Sin or no sin, Pharaoh's life certainly wasn't controlled by obedience to God. As long as the pace of life was moving along smoothly, God had no place in his thinking. He could "use the language" (28), but it made no impression on his heart or life.

● **"Repent when it can't be helped!"** After some particularly bad consequences of living without God, shock brings Pharaoh to repentance — quite regularly. But if it doesn't lead to a change in behavior, can you *really* call it repentance?

Think ● Moses sums it up. *"I know that you do not yet fear the Lord God"* (30). Does this say anything to you? Playing games with God shows that we don't yet honor him — not really, deep down.

Pray

that Christ may very deeply change your thinking and living.

Keynote

"I have sinned" (27) — "he sinned yet again" (34)

The Locust Crisis

● **Bargaining with God.** People like to bargain so much that they even try to bargain with God! Pharaoh, faced with an invasion of locusts, says, yes, "Let the men go" — *but* leave the women and children behind as hostages! People still bargain with God today.

"Lord, I will serve you, IF..." — if you get me out of this mess; if you heal my wife; if you help me through this exam; if you give us a child; if you get this plane down safely...

"Lord, I will serve you, BUT..." — but don't ask me to be a missionary; but don't ask me to stay single; but don't make me clean up my business; but don't ask me to love my father...

Why is it particularly wrong to bargain with God?

● **The Lord of nature acts.** But Pharaoh was trying to bargain with God, who is the Lord of Nature. In the plague of locusts, God used the forces of nature against the Egyptians. Locusts had been breeding in Arabia; a drought forced them to seek food elsewhere, a strong east wind carried them to Egypt! Coincidence?

Did "coincidence" bring the judgment? Pharaoh didn't think so (16)!

Did "coincidence" bring the blessing? Pharaoh didn't think so (17)!

Pray

that God will order the course of this world for the good of Christ's Kingdom.

Keynote

Winds of God

All or Nothing

"This is where you sign your life away!" said a friend of mine as a new bride sat down to sign the church register. And he was right. If you hold anything back, you deny your love and make a mockery of your marriage. And so it is when you become a Christian: you sign yourself over to Christ, you make a *complete commitment* to him. What's this got to do with today's passage? In it, you have examples of:

● **Token commitment.** Pharaoh seemed to have decided to go God's way, didn't he (24)? "Yes, you may go, with your women and children, too, just as the Lord has said." But — with a condition, *"Only let your flocks and herds remain behind!"* He was holding back enough to make the whole "commitment" useless.

● **Total commitment.** Moses' attitude is the exact opposite (26). *"Not a hoof shall be left behind!"* "We're taking everything with us. We've no idea what our commitment is ultimately going to involve, so we'll hold everything ready for the Lord!" That's true commitment — for the Christian, too.

Think ● **Why do you think some Christians try to give the Lord less than the whole of their lives? Lack of true love for Christ? Too much liking for non-Christian ways of living? Or what?**

Pray

that your devotion to Jesus Christ may be complete and sincere.

Keynote

"Not a hoof...''!

Stubbornness Is Weakness

What do you make of Pharaoh here? He knows he's beaten — no doubt about that. Now he's warned of a terrible disaster coming upon him and his people — he knows it will come, but he refuses to budge. He is a model of stubbornness for all time.

● **The reason for his obstinacy.** The reason is that he is maintaining an *appearance* of great strength. He sits on the throne, he's the great sovereign of the land, he's worshiped as a god. He thinks that to change his mind or give in would be a show of weakness that would spoil his image with the people. (Sound up-to-date?)

● **The results of his obstinacy.** To prove a point, and keep up his show, he's going to spread distress throughout his land. Not only will *he* suffer, but every other Egyptian family.

Note this: To be inflexible, to "make up one's mind and stick to it," is not always a sign of a strong character but often a weak one. You may bring suffering on yourself, your family, and many others, and you fool yourself that it's for the sake of a principle; but all the time it's just *fear* that people may think you're weak.

Think ● *True* strength is to find out the Lord's will in any situation, and do it, whatever people say.

Pray

that God will show you whether you are trying to put up a false front.

Keynote

The (apparently) strongest may be the (actually) weakest.

On to Freedom!

VERSE
OF THE WEEK
Exodus 12:13

We've begun the greatest chapter in the history of the people of Israel. What makes it especially interesting is that it is a deliberate illustration of what happens to *us* when we trust in Jesus Christ. Look again!

● **The end of the old life.** What was the "old life" for the Israelite people? It was a life of *slavery* and *despair*. Surely the "old life" for us is the slavery to our lusts, ambitions, confusion; it is the despair of ever gaining a purpose in life, or becoming what we knew we should. Now, in Christ that's all at an end.

● **The beginning of the new life.** Note that the Israelites had their meal with their sandals on and their walking sticks in their hands. You see, this wasn't just the end of the old, it was the beginning of the new! They had to be ready for it. Are you walking happily in the new life of freedom Jesus has given to you?

● **Between the two lives there was THE BLOOD ON THE DOORPOSTS.** Look at it this way: the lamb died instead of the "first-born" (or eldest son) of each family. And Christ, the perfect "Lamb of God," dies for *us,* so that we might be God's children, free in spirit!

Think ● What kinds of "death" have *we* been saved from?

Thank God

with all your heart for bringing you into the liberty of a new life.

Keynote

"For you — the beginning"!

Firm Anchors for Faith

I suppose we celebrate our birthdays each year to remind ourselves that we really were born, not found under a bushel!

Be that as it may, the Israelite people celebrated the *Passover* every year (17-18), to remind themselves that *it really happened* — they really were set free from their life of slavery into glorious liberty with their God!

For Christians, *the Lord's Supper* (or holy communion) has a similar meaning, a regular reminder that *it really happened* — we really have been set free from an old life and brought into the new! Both the Passover and the Lord's Supper, are *relived* by those who participate.

At the Passover and at the cross there are two parts:

● **What God did.** *For the Israelites:* Kept safe by the blood of a lamb, they had been delivered from Egypt by the mighty hand of God. *For us:* God gave us Jesus Christ, crucified at Calvary, to deliver us from the evil that dominated us.

● **What the people did.** *The Israelites:* They obeyed, they followed, they stepped out, trusting in the Lord. *The Christians:* We turned to Christ, put our trust in him, committed ourselves to his Kingdom.

Prayer

Lord, may I take these truths with me as I participate in the Lord's Supper.

Keynote

Lest we forget...

Beware of Complacency!

Pharaoh disastrously misjudged the Lord. He thought the Lord was too weak to bring such a judgment on the mighty Egyptian nation. So he did nothing when he should have been confessing how evil he had been, and obeying God.

People are always misjudging God. They don't believe that God will punish wrongdoing; they think he's too weak to do any such thing; they imagine God's heart will soften at the end and let them off. How devastatingly wrong!

● **Don't be careless about God's warnings!** Does verse 29 seem hard to live with? If so, is it because we've become *soft* in our morals? What the verse teaches is that God takes evil in people *deadly seriously,* and if they won't change they will suffer the consequences.

● **Don't be careless about God's commands!** These were very specific (21,22). Following these instructions was the *only* way to avoid the destruction coming on Egypt (23). God's finger is now pointing to the Christ of the Cross. He alone is "the Way, the Truth, and the Life" (John 14:6). You can't ignore him.

Think ● Is there something you think you can "get away with" in spite of what you know God thinks about it?

Pray

for all who think God is too weak to be taken seriously.

Keynote

He said it and did it

A Night to Remember

Do you remember one special night? Chances are it was a special night because it represented something *permanently new* in your life. It was a new beginning.

Today we read about "a night to be much observed" (42, KJV), one the Israelites never forgot. It was the night of their deliverance.

Do you remember a night (or perhaps a day) when Jesus Christ became real to you and you began a new life? Maybe you can't remember the date, but you know it happened. You'll find it similar to this story.

● **The departure was urgent!** Things had been getting worse for years (40). They were becoming unbearable. Then you heard a word from God, and your heart went out to Christ. The old life was left behind.

● **The journey lay ahead!** They "journeyed from Rameses to Succoth" (37). It was a *short* journey, hardly to the borders of Egypt. What a long way they had to go! *But it was a start.* You've probably come a long way since that day, and have a way to go; *but you are on the road!*

Think ● Have you come out of *your* "Egypt" yet? Have you been set free? Do you belong to God? Are you on the Christian road?

Pray

that today you may walk joyfully with Christ, and share him with someone else.

Keynote

Look back — then look on!

Keeping Faith Alive

Many experiences lay ahead of the Jews, and their faith would be severely tested. Hard times and easy times can *both* have a bad effect on our faith in Christ. It is really helpful, as Moses said, to "remember" (3). Some helps are:

● **Communion** — the holy communion, or Lord's Supper, is the memorial of Christ's death for our salvation, begun by the Lord himself.

● **Conversation** — talking with other Christians about what the Lord has done for us and them helps crystallize God's blessings.

● **Consideration** — to think back over the work of Christ in your life keeps things in perspective.

Today's passage points to two things we should "remember." (a) *Why we needed God to rescue us:* once a year "leaven" had to be deliberately put away, as a reminder that God has to "put away" our sins. (b) *What it cost God to rescue us:* the need to "redeem" every first son was an indication of what it would cost God to rescue us from sin — the life of his only Son.

Think ● What experiences have you had that assure you that Christ is alive and that you belong to him?

Praise God

for giving Jesus Christ as the ransom for your life.

Keynote

A high price to pay

God's Tender Care

You've probably heard the expression "T.L.C." It's "tender loving care," and we all need lots of it to survive! And the best place to get it is suggested in the title of this note.

It is helpful to read the New English Bible translation of part of verse 19, *"God will show his care for you."* Look a bit more closely.

● **God cares for you in spite of your faithlessness.** The Israelite people kept losing their faith. They kept complaining. They kept falling into sin. *Still God cared!*

● **God cares for you enough to handle you gently.** Verses 17-18 are very reassuring. God knew the Israelites couldn't take the strain of war at that point, so he led them around another way. "He will not test you further than you can bear..." (1 Corinthians 10:13). *Count on that!*

● **God cares for you and guides you day and night.** "To give them light" (21); they needn't walk in darkness, not even at midnight! God's sure but secret guidance is a blessing for each of his children.

Think ● **God's care is always there for everyone who is his own. The only condition: in spite of all our failures, a true desire to be on his side, and a humble faith in Jesus Christ.**

Pray

that you may be aware of God's care over you, and walk confidently.

Keynote

"To give them light"

It's Easy to Miscalculate

Except for Moses, everyone in today's story was miscalculating badly, and this led them to act in the wrong way.

● **The Lord, the forgotten factor** — was forgotten by the Egyptians. After all Pharaoh had seen of the Lord's power, he changed his mind again and came charging after God's people (5).

● **The Lord, the forgotten factor** — was forgotten by the Israelites! After all they had seen the Lord do for them, they seemed to forget, and fell into gloom and depression (10-12). In a way, it's not surprising, considering what they *saw* (10)! But there was One whom they could *not* see (14).

● **The Lord, the forgotten factor** — is he forgotten in the '70s? In many ways we would have to say "yes." Many people are now determining what is *right* and *wrong* for them without any reference to God's will or laws at all. Even some Christians are being carried along with this trend. Nations are being run without consideration for justice and with little concern for the underprivileged. And many people are becoming depressed, forgetting that the Lord is still around and far from "dead."

Think ● Live today with your eyes on the invisible Lord!

Pray

that the Lord's will may be put first, in your own life and in the life of your nation.

Keynote

"Stand firm" (13)

It Makes a Difference

**VERSE
OF THE WEEK
Exodus 14:14**

It made a tremendous difference whether you were an Israelite or an Egyptian! To be specific:

● **The Israelites had light; the Egyptians had darkness.** The "cloud" was different for each of them; a guiding light for Israel, a wall of darkness for the others. So for some people God is a light and a joy while to others he is a horror.

● **The Israelites had dry land; the Egyptians had the sea.** There's a real truth in this. People who trust God find him working wonderfully in everything; for those who are against him, even nature itself can be an enemy. God's people see God's hand in God's world.

● **The Israelites were saved; the Egyptians were lost.** It's in verse 30. It seems hard but God is firm.

It still makes a difference which side you are on. For those who don't care for God, life has a kind of built-in horror. It breaks out from time to time as they realize where their lives are heading. For those who have found God through Christ, the word is full of miracles. God is still hard at work.

Think ● **Did God love the Egyptians? If so, can you explain why he treated them that way?**

Pray

that through the efforts of his church, God will cause many people to change to his side.

Keynote

Reap as you sow

Your Introduction to Psalms 1-3

The Psalms are the prayer-and-hymnbook of ancient Israel. They consist of a collection of prayers written over several hundred years beginning with the poetic genius and remarkable spiritual insight of King David. Over the years many others contributed to the Psalter. The headings were mostly added long after the Psalms were written, on the basis of their use in Temple worship; they are not intended as exact statements of authorship.

The Psalter is remarkable because it allows us a glimpse into the religious experience and feelings of the Hebrews. The Psalms were written not only by kings but also by ordinary people like you and me. They range from confident praise of the great Lord to nagging questions about why he "hides his face," seeming to desert us. Here you will find praise, thanksgiving, suffering, depression, wisdom, and sheer delight as God's people seek to obey and understand him day by day.

Psalm 1 sets the tone of the whole Psalter. There are two ways to live one's life: in fellowship with the Lord and his people, or in fellowship with those who have rejected him. The latter course is folly and doom.

Psalm 2 proclaims the Lord as ruler over nations. He rules them through his anointed Son, the Messiah, and all nations are subject to him. This Psalm is fulfilled by Jesus Christ before whom "every knee shall bow"(Phil. 2:10).

Psalm 3 relates the experience of a warrior, very possibly David, who is about to be overwhelmed by the enemy. He cries out to God for help and obtains it.

As you read the Psalms, you too will be reminded of the wisdom of obeying God, God's sovereign rule over this world, and his care for you in both suffering and joy. With the Psalmist you, too, can "praise the Lord!"

Feeding Your Mind

The truth behind this psalm is that what you DO depends on what you ARE, and what you ARE depends on WHAT YOU FEED YOUR MIND.

"Get your defenses up." Verse 1 isn't suggesting we should *cut ourselves off* from "sinners," or have nothing to do with them, but that we shouldn't allow them to *mold our characters.* We are not to *walk* as they do (that is, go along with their standards), *stand* where they do (follow their example), or *sit* in their seat (adopt their pagan point of view). You must be on guard all the time against the pressure to conform.

"Get your Bible out!" If you resist the influences of society around you, you must have something to put in its place. Look at verse 2. To take time with the Bible will mold your thinking in *God's* way (3). If you wonder what "meditate" means, the *Guide for Daily Worship* at the front of these notes will give you a pretty good idea. It's worth using each day.

Think ● **Figure out what influences you most. Persuasive advertising? "The Joneses?" Avant-garde movies? Business pressures? Are they *good* influences?**
● **What priority does the Bible have in your life?**

Pray

that Jesus Christ may control your thinking and living.

Keynote

Food for thought

Honor the King!

As you read the *Psalms,* you'll find many of them seem to be speaking of Jesus Christ. Although they were written hundreds of years before he came, they point forward to him.

Psalm 2 is like that. Actually, it's about how the rulers of all nations were getting ready to fight against God's chosen king, David. But there is a deeper meaning in it. God's true "King" is Jesus.

Today the world has many more rulers than just *national* rulers. We have "rulers" of industry, of science, of commerce, of education, of labor, and what-have-you. Christ has few friends among them, just as in the olden days (1-2). In fact, they look on Christ and his way as so many shackles to be cast off (3). Times haven't changed.

How foolish these people look, when seen from heaven (4)! God has made his Son, Jesus, the rightful Lord of every part of human endeavor (6-8): space programs, exploration, research projects, unions of nations — all of them. Leave Christ out and you are headed for less than the best (10-12).

Think ● **You don't touch *all* of life, but you do touch *some* of it. How can you help bring *your* part under Christ's control?**

Pray

that the day may soon come when Christ's Lordship will be recognized all over the world.

Keynote

Lord of all life

To Be Able to Sleep

This is another situation which we can put in modern terms. David is surrounded by foes; soon they'll get him down and he'll be finished (1,2). And today? Your foes may not be murderers, but perhaps they are:

— **Doubts** or intellectual problems which bombard your mind.

— **Friends** whose attitude to you grows distinctly cool.

— **Family.** Jesus said that a "person's worst foes may be members of his own family."

— **Problems** ganging up to the point where you're losing control.

So you become afraid. You lie awake thinking, worrying, tossing and turning. *But not David* (5-6). How come?

(a) *Because he* believed *that the Lord would look after him* (3). Could you take what you know about the Lord and apply it to yourself?

(b) *Because he* prayed *that the Lord would look after him* (4,7). Try talking to the Lord through the day (aloud, if you're alone).

Think ● **Many today say God is irrelevant (2). Does verse 4 suggest how to answer them?**

Pray *for the gift of sound sleep, and thank God for it.*

Keynote **Sleeping or waking — safe**

Your Introduction to Acts

Luke's Good News: Part II is the lively account of the planting and growth of the young Church. *Part I* is what we call *The Gospel According to Luke;* it is a mistake to separate this too widely from its sequel, *Acts.* **Both Parts are about what Jesus Christ did on earth:** the first part when he was present in the flesh, the second part when he was present in the Person of the Holy Spirit. **Like a stone thrown into a pool,** the gift of the Holy Spirit at Pentecost (Acts 2) caused a series of spreading circles as the Church grew and expanded. We can outline *Acts* as follows:

I. Preparation for Pentecost: chapter 1

II. The Spirit is Given: chapter 2

III. Growth at Jerusalem: 3:1-8:3

IV. On to Samaria and Antioch: 8:4-12:25

V. Through the Empire with Paul: 13:1-38:31

   (1) 1st Missionary Journey: 13:1-14:28

   (2) Conference at Jerusalem: 15:1-35

   (3) 2nd Missionary Journey: 15:36-18:22

   (4) 3rd Missionary Journey: 18:23-21:6

   (5) To Rome as Prisoner: 21:7-28:31

Our Notes for the next three weeks will cover the first seven chapters of Acts.

Christ's Last Instructions

The keynotes of Acts. Acts is about Jesus and what he continued to do after he left the earth. It reflects the teaching which the risen Lord gave to his apostles. The Teacher through whom he spoke was the Person who dominates the events in this book — the Holy Spirit (8).

The opening scenes of Acts. This passage teaches us much about Jesus Christ.

(a) He definitely rose again from the grave (3) and proved it by a series of appearances to his disciples.

(b) He said a great deal about the "kingdom," or rule of God (3), just as he did in the Gospels.

(c) He expected absolute obedience from his disciples (4) — does he get it from us?

(d) He rebuked his disciples for expecting the wrong thing (6-7).

(e) He did not go back on his plan to use them, in spite of their mistake (8).

(f) He "ascended into heaven" (9). Modern ideas about space make this a difficult idea to understand. But how else could it have been made clear that he had gone back to be with his heavenly Father?

(g) He will return to the world again — visibly and triumphantly (11).

Question

The last words of Jesus were a command — "to the end of the earth" (8). Now in this century all the means for carrying out this order are available — what prevents it from happening?

Keynote

"With one accord...prayer" (14)

Small Group with a Big Mission

The small company. "About a hundred and twenty" (15) — God's cause in the world rested at this moment in the hands of this little group of unknown people in a small corner of the Roman Empire. Look up the good comment on this in Corinthians 1:26-28. What is more, these 120 seem to have been the net results of Jesus Christ's three years of preaching and healing — not much, by human standards! Judging things by quantity is not God's way: he goes for quality every time.

The twelve. Judas' loss was keenly felt. The number twelve was important — because when he was on earth Jesus had chosen twelve to be with him in a special way. So they had to choose another.

What Peter thought about the Old Testament — "the scripture...which the Holy Spirit spoke..." (16). For him, it was quite simply the inspired Word of God, which had to come true sooner or later. Remember, Peter had had the benefit of the finest Bible teaching ever given in all history. Who taught him? (Luke 24:44-45).

The two important things about an apostle — he had to have been one of Jesus' disciples from the beginning (21), so that he knew him well, and he had to be able to give first-hand evidence of the resurrection (22).

Prayer

Make me an effective witness this day, Lord, wherever I may go and to whomever I meet. Amen.

Keynote

"Lord, who knowest the hearts" (24)

They Were All Filled

Five times in chapter 1 the Holy Spirit is referred to — preparing the way for this central moment in the story of the Gospel of the Church and of the world itself. Pentecost was the Jewish "harvest festival" but *this* "harvest" was very different from an ordinary one. Jesus had died, like a seed (John 12:24), on the cross. Now the harvest — God's harvest — began to appear.

It was a harvest of power — "a mighty wind," "tongues as of fire" (2-3). This was the powerful combination which nothing could stop. Flames fanned by the wind sweep all before them. The cross appeared to be an act of weakness in the face of human sin, but God was not defeated.

It was a harvest of truth — "we hear...in our own tongues the mighty works of God" (11). The Holy Spirit's "tongues of fire" resulted in his servants being given tongues for teaching. They did not stop to discuss what was happening to them; they got on with the job of sharing the good news with others.

It was a harvest of the world (9-11). From all parts of the Empire, Jews and Gentiles ("proselytes," 10) saw and heard the miracle. Truth in power for the world — this is the hallmark of the Holy Spirit at work. Is it the hallmark of our own lives?

Prayer

Fill Your servants with the Holy Spirit today, Father, that the Good News of Jesus Christ may be made plain everywhere. Amen.

Keynote

"Filled with the Holy Spirit" (4)

Peter's Sermon

**VERSE
OF THE WEEK**
Acts 2:17

Peter preaches the first evangelistic sermon of the Christian Church. Note that it was listened to with great attention because it followed upon something that happened. The best introduction to a sermon is not a funny story, but an *event* which makes people ask, "What does all this mean?"

The promise fulfilled. Peter's message begins with a reference to an Old Testament prophecy; verses 17-21 are a direct quotation from the prophet Joel (2:28-32). It concerns,

(a) *What God will do* ("Pour out my Spirit," 17; "show wonders," 19).

(b) *What men may do as a result* ("Call on the name of the Lord...be saved," 21).

The Person exalted. Verse 22 comes to the central point, "Jesus..." *He* is the Gospel. God had done "mighty works" in him. Men had answered with a typically rebellious deed — the cross (23). "But God..." (24) had the last word. Another prophecy, this time from a psalm of David (16:8-11), had come true.

Prayer

Make verses 25-28 your own prayer today.

Keynote

"But God..."

Other Testimony to Christ

David foretells Christ's resurrection and ascension. In Peter's audience were Jews and Gentiles who knew a good deal about Jewish religion. So King David was the hero of them all. Peter here makes it clear that in Psalm 16 (verses 25-28 in today's passage) David could not have been forecasting his own resurrection: he was speaking of Christ (30). Neither did David "ascend" into heaven (34). So another of his prophecies, from Psalm 110, must have been about Christ.

Peter uses Christ's prophetic names. Peter calls him *"Jesus"* (32) — it is his *human* name. *"The Christ"* (31) refers to him as the *Son of God*. It means "the anointed One," particularly the One who was to fulfill God's promises to Israel, the *Messiah* for whom the Jews were waiting. *"Lord"* (36) refers to him as the *King of all the earth*.

If you are puzzled about the idea of the Trinity, about God as "Three-in-One," look carefully at verse 33. Jesus Christ the "Son" receives from the "Father" the promised "Holy Spirit" whom he gives to his disciples. All three are at work in the Pentecost event, the birthday of the Christian Church. The Spirit makes Jesus Christ real to us, so that we may know and serve the Father.

Prayer

Pour out in my life this day, O God, the fullness of the Holy Spirit to the praise of Christ. Amen.

Keynote

"Lord and Christ..."

"What Shall We Do?"

The sermon finishes... (37-42). "What does this mean?" (13) had become "What shall we do?" (37). It's one thing to discuss the meaning of the Gospel, it's a very different thing to feel the truth being applied to us personally, making a demand upon us — which is what it does. When the Holy Spirit gets to work it is the *second* question that men ask — and the answer is clear, "Turn away from your sins...and be baptized in the name of Jesus Christ" (38, TEV).

There is a negative step — "turn from" — for if you want to hold on to things which go against God's will, you cannot open your hands to receive God's gifts.

There is a positive step — "be baptized" — that is, openly commit yourself to the people of God in the act of baptism that shows how he is willing to forgive and receive you. Following this, Peter explains what happens as we obey this call — see verse 38.

...But does not end. Verses 43-47 show how the Pentecost message went on spreading its influence. Too many sermons stop at the doorway of the church, and we never give them a chance to go on working outside. These early Christians simply could not be suppressed. Their new life showed through in the way they handled their property (45), ate their meals (46), and worshiped God.

Prayer

May the truth which has come to me in this reading show clearly in everything I do and say today. Amen.

Keynote

"Glad and generous hearts" (46)

More Than He Asked For

The Temple and the beggar. The Temple was the center of Jewish religion and worship, but the best it could do for the lame man was to provide a place for begging. What a picture this is of a church from which the true life of God has departed! But God was at work in Jerusalem, not in the Temple priests and learned scribes, but in those Galilean fishermen and their friends who were filled with the Holy Spirit. Notice, however, that they had not abandoned the Temple: it still stood for the true God, even though the Jews had rejected Christ.

The apostles and the beggar. The beggar had gotten so used to his weakness that he expected nothing more than money. One of the things that happens to people who get into bondage to evil is that they lose hope.

But this day is different! Peter and John are not just another pair of time-serving Temple priests: they are full of the Spirit, friends and witnesses of the living Christ. They have no money (6) — you don't need a fortune to care for needy people. Imagine how the beggar's face changed: "Silver and gold...none" — his face falls, his lips curl sullenly. "Such as I have I give..." — puzzled, cynical frown. "In the name ...walk" — doubt, astonishment, caution, rapture — he got much more than he ever asked for!

Prayer

Lord, help me not to settle for less than God's best for me, or to give less than his best to others.

Keynote

"Walking and praising God"

Peter Explains

The wrong hero (11,12). We talk nowadays about the "personality cult" — in which outstanding people become the center of attention and influence. It happens with TV stars, sportsmen, and in religion as well. So the healed man "clung" to Peter and John (11), and the crowd swarmed around them.

The right perspective (13-16). Peter quickly puts them straight. It had all begun with God and the things that he had done through Jesus Christ (13), in spite of the Jews and their opposition (14). Note that Peter doesn't hesitate to tell them that they are guilty in God's sight.

Finally, Peter explains the real secret — "his name" (16). The "name" here stands for everything that Jesus represents; just as a military officer will act "in the President's name." It stands for authority and order. So the "name" of Jesus stands for all the authority of God working through his Spirit.

The real issue (17-26). "And now" — Peter doesn't just explain events — he applies the truth directly to the crowd. This time it is Moses whom he quotes, followed up by references to Samuel and Abraham. Devout Jews, experts in the Old Testament, would get the force of all this. The message is the same as before — see verses 19 and 26.

Prayer

"Forth in Thy name, O Lord, I go..."; may I not dishonor You today. Amen.

Keynote

"His name...has made this man strong"

You Can't Imprison Truth

The establishment runs true to form (1-4). Religious organizations, like the Temple system, don't take kindly to "unofficial" action by people who haven't been recognized or approved. In spite of the evidence of the beggar and dozens of witnesses to the miracle, they lock up Peter and John. In the same way, we all try to hide or suppress things which don't fit into our tidy traditional systems. Human beings just don't like change.

The new men keep up the attack (5-12). A very solemn and frightening Jewish court assembles to "try" the "offenders." Old, learned, very powerful — they are the high court of the nation. But the question they ask (7) reveals that either they had not bothered to get the facts, or else that they were hoping to trap Peter and John into saying something that would put them in trouble. They knew very well "by what name" it had all happened.

But Peter is not going to be bullied: he goes straight to the attack — "by the name of Jesus Christ of Nazareth, whom you crucified." This was the very court that had sentenced Jesus Christ to death, and from which Peter had once run away. Why is he now so bold? See verse 8 for his secret.

Prayer

O God, there is no one else in all the world but Jesus through whom men can be saved from their sins. I trust in him alone and I ask that my life may make him better known today. Amen.

Keynote

"There is salvation in no one else" (12)

You Can't Frighten Faithful Men

Men of religion (13-18). The all-powerful court, called the Sanhedrin, is now a group of confused and frightened men.

The judges were surprised (13): Peter and John were "uneducated, common men" — they had not had a college education, and their whole style was rough and unpolished. But they had what really mattered — they were certain of God, and they had their evidence with them (14).

The judges were puzzled (16): "What shall we do?" the Jewish leaders asked. This would be a good question if it came from people who were ready to receive the truth (see 2:37). But on this occasion it simply revealed that they had made up their minds to suppress the Gospel, and were angry because they could not find a way to do it.

The judges were baffled: "We cannot deny it!" And so, like bullies everywhere, they tried to frighten the apostles into silence (18). They still had not realized that they were dealing with:

Men of faith (19-22). You can't frighten a man who is sure of God and who can speak of what he has "seen and heard" (20). The Church tends to get into a vicious circle; nothing much happens, so faith withers, so even less happens! How is this circle broken? See 1:8 for the answer.

Prayer

Strengthen my faith, O God, through Your Word, Your Son, Your Spirit, and through circumstances which seek to suppress Your truth.

Keynote

"What we have seen and heard"

Prayer and Practical Christianity

VERSE
OF THE WEEK
Acts 4:32

Sometimes people talk as if they had to choose between being the kind of Christian who concentrates on witnessing for Christ and praying to God, and the kind who goes in for doing practical deeds of kindness and service. But these early Christians were *both*. See how it worked out here.

A prayer meeting that shook things (23-31). Notice what they put into their prayer (they didn't worry about the threat that had been made, 21; they left the bullies in God's hands).

They begin with God the Creator (24).

They think of God the Revealer — whose truth is in the Scriptures (25,26).

They see God the Fulfiller of promises (27), especially in Christ.

They remember God the Controller of all that happens (28).

Their prayer so far is more concerned with God than with what they want. How do our prayers compare?

A practical obedience that united people (32-37). They share their possessions and they preach with great success — these go together. The love of Christ, where he is really at work, unlocks purses *and* opens lips.

Prayer

So often, Lord, we neither pray nor do we put our Christianity into practice. Fill us with the Holy Spirit that we may be effective in all directions in Your service. Amen.

Keynote

"Everything in common"

Fatal Dishonesty

What a tremendous time it was to be a Christian! "Yes," you say, "if I had been there, I wouldn't have been the half-hearted, timid, feeble Christian that I am. I'd have been right in there with the apostles and the others..." Are you *sure*?

Keeping good company doesn't make us good. Even when "revival" is in full flood, when the church is fully alive in the power of the Spirit, Christians can lie and cheat and deceive. So it depends on what we are in our inward attitude to God. There was a Judas among Christ's disciples, and an Ananias in the early church.

Deceiving the Lord brings judgment. Ananias was not *compelled* to sell the field. The sharing among the Christians was voluntary. There are no rules about what Christians should or should not give away, for "love fulfills the Law," and when Christ is in control then rules become unnecessary. But Ananias tried to keep face with the apostles and appear noble, while keeping back a part of the proceeds.

So the same voice that had brought healing to the lame man (3:6) brings judgment and doom to the deceivers; just as one and the same Voice gave gracious invitations (Matthew 11:28-29) and issued terrible warnings (Luke 11:42-44).

Prayer

I thank You, Lord, for the reminder that I cannot deceive You. Make me absolutely honest today in all my dealings. Amen.

Keynote

No holding back

Growth and Opposition

The believers increase (12-16). It was a great and exciting time to be involved in the Christian community! It all fulfilled Christ's promise in John 14:12 (look this up).

But did you notice how verse 14 seems to contradict verse 13? Did more people join the Christians or didn't they? Look at it more carefully. Verse 13 says "none...dared join them" — that is, people just couldn't make up their minds to become Christians as they would join any other group; it was too solemn and costly a thing for that. But verse 14 says "believers were added to the Lord." Something took hold of people, almost in spite of themselves, and led them to faith in Christ. C.S. Lewis described himself as dragged "kicking and squealing into the Kingdom...!"

The Sadducees react (17-26). "If you can't deny the truth, lock up the witnesses" is the policy of tyrants. The religious leaders should have been glad that so many sufferers were healed. But jealousy puts mirrors instead of windows in our hearts so that we see only ourselves and what we are losing. So they put the apostles in prison.

Miraculously released, the apostles went back to their preaching. What they preached was a "Life" (20) — that is, a way of living, in obedience to Christ.

Prayer

I thank You, Lord, for taking hold of my life. Make me a lively and happy Christian. Amen.

Keynote

"The Lord opened the prison doors"

Obeying God Rather Than Men

The apostles cannot be silenced (27-32; 40-42). When they are put on trial (27-32), Peter takes the opportunity (30,31) to preach that:

(a) a real man was crucified on a real cross,

(b) he rose again from the dead,

(c) God was at work in all that happened,

(d) it was all connected with Israel's past; it was done by the "God of our fathers" (30),

(e) Christ has ascended to glory,

(f) the response men should make is to repent,

(g) the benefit to men is sins forgiven,

(h) those who do respond receive the Holy Spirit, God's gift.

The Truth cannot be overthrown (33-39). Again the Jewish leaders try to suppress the truth. But Gamaliel (the teacher of a well-known young Pharisee, 22:3) reminded them that fighting against God is a waste of time.

Christian joy cannot be suppressed (40-42). Verse 41 is worth thinking over: even being persecuted becomes a source of joy for the Christian. Here were people who loved Christ so much that everything that happened was put to good use in his service.

Pray

for such a certainty of God that nothing can silence your witness or rob you of your joy.

Keynote

"Dishonor for the name" (41)

Christian Problem Solving

The "Hellenists" were Jewish Christians with a background of Greek language and culture; the "Hebrews" were the stricter Jewish Christians who tended to hold on to their rigid Jewish religion and way of life. Although the big outreach to Gentiles had not yet begun, the young Church was already being threatened by this dispute between the two groups. It plays a large part in the history of the Church in the New Testament.

The problem is stated in verse 1. The "distribution" was the sharing of food and other necessities. Some seemed to be more favored.

The danger was that the dispute could have taken up the time of the twelve apostles who had more important tasks (4). This still happens quite often in the Christian Church. Do people nowadays regard prayer in this way — a task that *must* be done?

The answer was a plan put forward by the apostles. But note that it was also approved by the Christians as a whole ("multitude," verse 5). Put verses 3 and 5 together and we see the three things they looked for in the men they appointed.

The results are spelled out clearly in verse 7. Note that "priests" were included — men who were on the staff of the Jewish leaders!

Prayer

Give to me, O God, Your gifts of wisdom and faith. But above all fill me this day with Your Holy Spirit. Amen.

Keynote

"Full of faith and of the Holy Spirit"

Stephen Accused

The clouds gather. So far the story has been one of unbroken success for the Gospel. Even the arrests and appearance before the Jewish Council had turned out for the good of the cause. But it could not go on much longer: after all, Jesus Christ himself had been cruelly executed by those same people — could his followers expect to escape trouble? Look up what he himself said about this — John 15:18-21.

The fight begins. It was only words at first — disputing and rousing the mob. But it was a real fight, for the Christian Gospel challenged some of the ideas which the Jews held very strongly. The Gospel said that you could not reach God's standard by obeying the Law, and that all men had to receive forgiveness through the cross. Most offensive of all, it said that Jesus of Nazareth, whom the Jews had crucified, was the Son of God. There could be no half-way position. So Stephen became the center of the storm.

The pattern is repeated. What happened to Stephen is similar to what they did to Christ. Make time tomorrow to read Luke's story of the cross (Luke 22:54 — 23:49) and see how many things are the same — the charge of blasphemy, the false witnesses, the mob, the lying accusation.

Prayer

Dear Lord, help me to know the meaning of the words, "It is the way the Master went — should not the servant tread it still?"

Keynote

"Crucified with Christ"

Stephen's Answer

The point of the Jewish charge against Stephen was that he had been attacking the Temple worship and the Laws of Moses. So he sets out to prove the opposite — namely, that Jesus Christ had come to *fulfill* the Old Testament, not to contradict it.

And what was more, the Gospel showed the true meaning of the Old Testament, just as an artist's finished painting shows what he really had in mind when he drew the first rough pencil sketches. This does not mean that the Old Testament is unimportant. But it does mean that we must always understand the Old Testament in the light of what the New Testament teaches.

As you read Stephen's speech in the next few days look out for certain points which he keeps emphasizing with this in mind. In particular, he is quietly emphasizing that the heroes of Jewish history had been:

(a) sent and strengthened by God;

(b) rejected by the Israelites.

In this way he will lead up to the point where he will charge his audience with being just like their ancestors. Can you see any hint of this in today's reading? Look at verse 9.

Prayer

I thank You for Your Word of Truth, O Lord; teach me how to understand it and how to put it to effective use. Amen.

Keynote

"The God of Glory"

God's Spokesmen

VERSE
OF THE WEEK
Acts 7:51

The Israelites' error. Stephen is steadily emphasizing his main point — *that the Jews had always misunderstood and rejected their leaders.* They honored them afterward, and made a great fuss about keeping up their traditions; but at the time, they treated them badly — even Moses, the greatest name in Jewish history. Twice Stephen makes the point; first in verse 25, where the people as a whole are blamed for not recognizing their deliverer; and again in verses 27-28, where two individual Israelites reject his help.

Stephen is preparing his hearers for the truth about their greatest rejection of all — the crucifying of Jesus Christ. The Jews boasted that Moses was their leader: but they conveniently forgot what had happened when he was alive. Christians still do this kind of thing.

Moses' choice. Stephen shows how Moses, who had enjoyed great privileges, had come to a moment of choice. He saw an Egyptian overseer bullying a Jewish slave — one of his own people. He made his choice — "He preferred to suffer with God's people rather than to enjoy sin for a little while" (Hebrews 11:25; look up what verse 26 says about his *motive*). Somewhere, sometime, every Christian has to make a choice of this kind.

Prayer

Help me to get my values right, O Lord, so that I may make wise choices in life. And give me the discernment to receive and believe those who speak of You. Amen.

Keynote

God has his man ready for every need

Moses Rejected

Now Stephen makes his point crystal clear. He is still talking about the greatest leader in Jewish history, Moses; and he is still moving toward the climax — where a greater leader than Moses suffered the same fate as Moses had experienced. So we have:

The revelation. It was not Moses' first-class education as a prince of Egypt that made him fit to lead God's people. What was it? — See verses 31-32. Education is good; but unless God reveals himself personally to us, we lack the most vital thing. And note how Moses responded (end of verse 32).

Then note how God proposes to help his people in their slavery — "I have come down to deliver them"; "I will send you" (34). Moses might have replied — "Do *you* intend to do it, or do you want *me* to?" But he knew that the truth lay in a blend of the two — *God* would act *through Moses,* his servant. That is God's method — to use men who know how to obey.

The rejection. Twice the Israelites rebelled against God's chosen servant — see verses 35 and 39. In the first place it was *pride* — "Why should you be leader?" In the second place it was *lack of faith and patience* — they wanted a god they could see, not the living God who spoke through Moses.

Prayer

Make me one of Your effective co-workers, Lord — able to interpret Your will and willing to do it. Amen.

Keynote

"The voice of the Lord came"

They Couldn't Stand the Truth

Stephen's outline of Jewish history suddenly gains speed — were his hearers showing signs of getting angry as they began to see what he was driving at? So (44-47) we have Moses, Joshua, David, and Solomon. The "house" (47) that Solomon built was the Temple. Stephen bravely puts all such buildings in their place (48). Then comes:

a) The direct accusation (51-53). Stephen's point is made: the Jews of Christ's day were the true successors of their ancestors — murderers of God's servants, rebels against God's truth. Yet they did not realize it. What are the blind spots of God's people today?

b) The open vision. Stephen, man of faith (6:8), could see deep into the hearts of men and far into the presence of God (56). These two often go together.

c) The bitter reaction. When the truth of God is made clear, people do not necessarily obey or even listen. How did the Jews react (54,57)? How do *you* react to truth that hurts?

d) The Christlike conclusion. Verses 59-60 are full of echoes of Calvary. A Roman centurion was impressed by the dying Lord Jesus; an even more important person was impressed by the dying Stephen — who was it (58)?

Prayer

Give courage, Lord, to all Your servants, especially those who have to cope with hostile authorities. Amen.

Keynote

"Heaven is my throne and earth my footstool"

Your Introduction to Judges

When did the story take place? After God had so miraculously delivered the Israelites from Egypt (Exodus), they wandered for 40 years in the desert and finally arrived in Canaan, the Promised Land. As the tribes of Israel were settling into their new homeland, they had little sense that they belonged together. Each tribe did more or less as it pleased. Israel was ruled by a series of "judges."

What happened in the story? Time and again the people became unfaithful to the Lord. They were attracted by the religions they found in the land, and kept following "Baal" and other heathen "gods." The result was that God refused to go on helping them, and they were conquered by other nations. This made them turn to God again (for a little while, anyway). Then the whole circle began again!

What does the story mean? The story of Judges gives one simple message over and over again. It is that to give up following the Lord leads to trouble, but to turn back to him brings deliverance. Life may seem much more complicated than that, but all the same it is a lesson we need to learn in a prosperous world that puts "other gods" around us every day.

Our readings in Judges will cover chapters 13-16, the story of Samson.

A Lesson in "Child Care"

(*In many ways, Manoah's child was a "special case." But we Christians can learn a lot here about bringing up children.*)

● **First principle:** *The child is a gift from God.* Nowadays we know all about "how babies are born"! But verse 3 looks at it from God's end. Our children are really his, and we look after them for him.

● **Second principle:** *The child must be prayed over BEFORE* he is born. Verses 8 and 12 show you Manoah's greatest concerns, which made him pray to the Lord before the baby arrived. It is never too *soon* to pray.

● **Third principle:** *The child must be given to God from birth.* What a mistake to let a child live without God until he gets old enough to go his own way! Look at verse 5. This child was to start young. How can we help our children to do the same?

● **Fourth principle:** *The child learns most by watching his parents.* This child was to get his first lessons in following the Lord from the example of his own mother (4,14). He would become what she became first.

The Home and the Child

Portrait of a God-centered home. What a home for the child to grow up in! Imagine:

● **Its unity** — the whole story shows the lovely spirit that existed between Manoah and his wife; they discussed everything together and served the Lord together.

● **Its hospitality** — they gave credit to others, not criticism (17).

● **Its worship** — the whole family joined in honoring the Lord (20).

● **Its faith** — the Lord's Word and the Lord's goodness were utterly trusted (17,23).

No wonder God chose this family as a home for his special servant!

Portrait of a God-centered child. The careful upbringing his parents gave him began to bear fruit even during Samson's childhood. We see him:

● **Growing in body** (24) — good food and exercise did their work.

● **Growing in knowledge** (24) — especially knowledge of the Lord.

● **Growing in experience** (25) — finding more and more of God's Spirit at work in his life.

Prayer

Lord, may we give a good start to the next generation by faithful, balanced Christian homes.

Keynote

Like father, like son

Be Yourself!

"Ordinary Christians" find it hard to get along with someone who is "different." Many good people are lost to the church simply because they can't toe all the party lines. Samson was an unusual person like that. We can imagine how frustrated his parents must have felt (3)!

● **"Samson, why don't you stick to the accepted way of doing things?** Marry a nice sensible Israelite girl like all the other boys, and settle down like the rest of us!" His parents were quiet, saintly people, as we have seen, and they couldn't bear to think of Samson becoming anything else. What didn't they know (4)?

● **"Samson, why do you keep shocking us?** We don't go around killing lions: we try to be respectable!" They couldn't tolerate his unorthodox ways. But the Lord doesn't want everyone the same. Samson was full of imagination and full of courage; God wanted to develop these gifts (6).

● **"Samson, why must you always 'go it alone'?** You could be so much more help if you would work in with the priests and the other religious leaders!" But why squeeze Samson into the usual mold? Some people are killed by that.

Prayer

Lord, help me to be MYSELF, and not to criticize others for being THEMSELVES too.

Keynote

All kinds to make a world

Does Samson Make Sense?

Did you end today's reading wondering, "Where on earth is the sense in *that?*" Rest assured, there is a great deal of sense in it! The clue to it all is that Samson was a man of enormous strength, and that *God was planning to use him singlehanded to break the evil power of the Philistines!* This thought will help us to answer some questions:

● **Why would God move Samson to ruin his own wedding?** Verse 4 answers this question. The whole "wedding" was a scheme to make trouble for the Philistines!

● **Why would God move Samson to pick a quarrel with his companions?** (For, of course, the riddle was meant to lead to a fight, whether or not they got it right.) The answer is that those 30 "companions" were in fact his deadly enemies. Samson brought the quarrel into the open, and got some action.

● **Why would God move Samson to kill 30 men (19)?** Because it was the next stage in the plan! It would reach the ears of the Philistine high-ups. They were infuriated and their anger drew them on to their own destruction.

Prayer

Lord, my life is so easy compared with all Samson went through. Make me willing to suffer for Your sake.

Keynote

Be a hero — for God!

A Wild Outcast

VERSE OF THE WEEK
Judges 16:20

Picture Samson now! His uncut hair flying in all directions, his eyes blazing, he fights alone against the hosts of the Philistines, then goes off to live as a cave man in the rock Etam (8). He is an outcast, lonely and despised —

- **hated** by the Philistines,

- **cut off** from his family,

- **unwanted** by his nation.

And yet — this is the amazing thing — he was in fact God's servant, in God's place for him, doing God's work. Through his efforts God's people would be set free from the Philistines for many years.

What can we learn from this? Surely that different Christians are called to different tasks and to be different kinds of people:

- **Some are called to argue, defend the faith,** attack error, stand for truth.

- **Others are called to talk quietly, persuade gently,** be sympathetic, help the needy.

And neither kind should look down on the other — 1 Corinthians 12:21!

Prayer

Save me, Lord, from thinking that every other Christian has to see things just the way I do.

Keynote

Christians are not mass-produced

A One-Man Campaign

Now you see why Samson could not work with the men of his own people (11). He could never have gotten them mobilized against the Philistines — it *had* to be a one-man campaign. And so you have:

● **The official sell-out.** The men of Judah no longer stood for God, for the Jewish faith, for the Scriptures. They had sold out to the Philistines for the sake of peace and quiet (11). Samson was a nuisance to them; he disturbed the peace; he wouldn't adjust to the situation!

● **The unofficial struggle.** One man filled with God's Spirit did more than 3,000 men without him (11,14)! He had no official position; in fact, the high-ups were glad to be rid of him (12); yet he dealt another mighty blow at Philistine power (15).

Question 1: Do you think that some churches are selling out the Christian faith by keeping too quiet about it?

Question 2: Do you think that a Christian who is filled with God's Spirit and takes a stand for Christ will be looked upon as a nuisance?

Question 3: Do you think God is calling you to speak out more bravely as a Christian?

Prayer

Let me not be a nuisance for the sake of being a nuisance, but may I always be bold to stand for Christ's Kingdom.

Keynote

Odd man out?

How Strong, Yet How Weak!

Samson's tragedy was that he never became master of his passions. Once again we see him manipulated by a designing woman: "Entice him!" (5).

Notice carefully this difference: Samson was right to insist on being "himself," and not to be forced into a mold; but he was wrong to give in to the demands of his own body. It's good to be an individual; it's bad to be a sinner. His service was spoiled. God could not use him fully. *But:*

● **How strong Samson was again!** Here is something worth remembering. God *does not abandon his children when they sin! Samson should not have been where he was in verse 1; but God gave him strength in verse 3 just the same! And even more amazing:*

● **How weak Samson was again!** Here he is, giving in to the same temptation. But think about this: *God worked even Samson's sin into his plan.* With one blow, Israel was going to be freed from 3,000 of the cream of the Philistines, including the five top overlords (30)! God could even turn Samson's stupidity to his own use. This is no excuse for Samson, but it does bring glory to God!

Prayer

Lord, make me what I should be. But meanwhile, use me as I am.

Keynote

"The secret of his strength" (9, RSV)

Daily Pressures

It's a strange fact that most of us can find the strength to face a great disaster, or dreadful pain, or an obvious temptation, and overcome it. But what gets us down is when life nags at us day after day, with no way to get away from it. Hear the devil wearing Samson down:

● **"Give in to the pressures!"** We say that constant dripping wears away a stone. At first Delilah's questions seemed like a joke, and Samson gave funny answers (10). But *"when she pressed him* with her words day after day" (16), Samson gave in. But he needn't have. There is no limit to the length of time a Christian can hold out, with God's strength.

● **"Give over your faith!"** "Stop thanking God for his mercy! Forget about your Bible! Don't bother with prayer any more!" That's the voice of Satan, for these are the very things that keep us close to our Lord. Samson gave them over.

● **"Give up your God!"** Samson betrayed his Lord and lost his power (17), but you need not. Each day is a fresh battle. Take fresh strength from God, and hold firm to the end.

Prayer

Lord, I find drudgery and monotony hard to face. Give me fresh joy in my heart, day after day.

Keynote

Life goes on and on. So does the Lord!

From Tragedy to Triumph

● **The greatest tragedy of Samson's life.**
Verse 20 is one of the most pathetic verses in the
Bible. Some Christian writers make Samson out
to be a great villain; others think he was one of
God's great heroes. But this makes his fall the
more tragic. He had let the Lord down the night
before, but he didn't realize that the Lord had
taken his strength away. It is a great mistake to
think that you can fail your Lord without
weakening your Christian life.

*Do you realize how little you can do for the
Lord in your own strength?*

● **The greatest triumph of Samson's life.** The
moment when he realized his strength was gone
must have been the most terrible of Samson's
life. But it showed him his great need of God, and
in the Philistine prison he turned his blinded
eyes to the Lord. For him, perhaps, it was just a
desire for personal vengeance (28), but God
brought far more out of his prayer than Samson
ever knew (30). You will never be able to measure
the influence your life will have, if you place it
back in God's hands.

*Do you realize how much you can do for the
Lord in God's strength?*

Prayer

*Lord, make me repentant, and keep me
obedient, and use my small life mightily.*

Keynote

"Remember me! Strengthen me!" (28)

Your Introduction to Romans

Paul had never visited Rome although he had a deep longing to meet the Christians there (15:23), and see results among them.

Romans is unique among Paul's Letters for its exposition of the Gospel and its implications for conduct and life. Paul found it necessary to correct situations in the Roman church and show his credentials as an apostle, so as to prepare the way for his long-hoped-for visit.

Three themes to look for. Chapters 1-8 contain the basic explanation of God's method of putting sinful men right with himself. Look out for three main themes, each marked by the word "Therefore."

The first is in 3:20-23 where Paul shows that everyone, Gentile and Jew, has sinned against God and is in danger of his *judgment.* The second comes in chapter 5, where we learn that *justification,* or release from the consequences of sin depends not on our efforts, but on faith in the work of Christ. Chapter 8, verse 1 highlights *sanctification,* which should result from our justification.

If you bear in mind these three words — judgment, justification, and sanctification — you will have the main guidelines through these remarkable chapters.

Man with a Message

● **From Paul...** (1). When Paul speaks of himself, it is often in two ways, playing down his person, and playing up his mission. We find it here. He was a "servant" (literally, "slave") of Jesus — a position of humility and inferiority and yet he was also "an apostle," an ambassador for his Master — a position of great privilege. Can you see how this applies to you?

● **About Jesus...** (3,4). This is the great subject of his letter, and here at the outset he writes of Jesus in two ways. He was *"Son of Man"* ("the flesh," 3) and also *"Son of God"* ("the spirit," 4). Jesus was not a man pretending to be God, nor was he God disguised as a man; but at one and the same time he was perfect man and perfect God. This great mystery is beyond our understanding. (Read Philippians 2:5-8).

● **To Rome** (6, 7). What sort of people was Paul writing to? You can read about some of them in chapter 16. We learn here (7) that they were "beloved by God" and "called saints," people reconciled to God through Christ, then consecrated to a life of holiness and service. We are saved to be separated; delivered to be dedicated.

Question: Do you have a message for the world around *you?*

Prayer

O Lord, make me grateful for what Jesus is and for all that he has done for me.

Keynote

"Called" from...by...to...

Missionary Concern

Paul reveals three activities in his life:

● **Praying (8-10).** We can learn much from Paul about how to pray. Notice these phrases — "I thank" (8), "without ceasing" (9), "the will of God" (10). Paul *mentioned people by name* (9) and then he *made specific requests* (10). His prayers were not vague and nebulous.

● **Visiting (11-12).** A large part of Paul's missionary concern involved visiting people, to give them strength, encouragement and instruction, in the name of Christ. Do you have this concern?

● **Preaching (13-15).** When we turn to Paul's preaching, there are two phrases which strike us:

"I am debtor" (14). "Surely you mean 'benefactor,' Paul!" "No, I *owe* people the Gospel. I am like a doctor with a life-saving drug in his bag. Woe to me if I do not preach the Gospel."

"I am ready" (15). Could you, at a moment's notice, and with the help of your Bible, explain Christ to someone? We should be able to take immediate advantage of every opportunity we are given.

Question: How real is *my* missionary concern?

Prayer

Lord, when I feel slack and lazy, help me to remember the debt I owe to my fellowmen, and make me ready for it.

Keynote

"Paul the ready"

Why Doesn't God Do Something?

**VERSE
OF THE WEEK
Romans 2:1**

As we look at the corruption in our world, we are apt to ask that question. Paul's answer in today's Note is: "He *is* doing something!"

● **He is revealing himself** (19,20). Proof of God's existence, power and glory are plain for every man to see and know in nature, the things God has so carefully made.

● **He is judging the wicked** (18). Those who reject God are without excuse, and their wicked behavior exposes them to the "wrath of God" (18).

● **He is redeeming the faithful** (16-17). In addition to his self-disclosure and judgment, God is exercising his righteousness and power:

The righteousness of God (17). Shouldn't Paul be speaking about "the love of God"? Why "the righteousness of God"? Because love by itself could never bring us redemption. It had to be love *and justice.* God could not simply overlook our sin. Someone (Christ) had to bear its burden and guilt; and where love and justice meet you get perfect righteousness.

The power of God (16). This news — the Gospel — has power to rescue and transform all who accept it by faith.

Question: Are you playing a part in "what God is doing"?

Prayer

O Lord, may that wonderful plan of redemption I see upon the cross inspire and humble me all through my life. Amen.

Keynote

"The righteousness of God"

He Gave Them Up...

● **The progress of sin.** In today's passage we are given a more detailed picture of man's corruption and God's angry judgment on it. We see the progress of sin, once it is let loose in a person's life. It begins in the *heart* (24) as unclean lusts and passions; then it reaches the *body* (24) which becomes the instrument of evil; and it ends in the mind (28) which becomes twisted and depraved, believing wrong is right.

● **The hostility toward God.** Alongside this increasing moral corruption, and indeed the cause behind it, we can trace a deepening hostility toward God:

He is rejected (21) by those who prefer to manage their own lives.

He is supplanted (22-25), for "nature abhors a vacuum," and if man will not have the true God, then he will find one of his own and worship that.

He is ignored (28), as life is organized without reference to him.

He is hated (30), and actively opposed.

There are no more solemn words than the thrice repeated verdict, "God...gave them up..." (24,26,28). To reject God means to be rejected by him; to deny him in this life, means to be denied by him in the next life.

Prayer

O Lord, occupy the center of my life, and arrest the progress of sin. Amen.

Keynote

"Given up"

God's Judgment

● **It applies to everyone.** You can almost imagine a Jew nodding his head with approval at Paul's awful description of human sinfulness in 1:18-32. But, "Beware!" cries Paul. "Don't set yourself up as a judge of other men." The Jew could easily think that his nation's long relationship with God's goodness gave him an immunity from God's judgment.

But such an attitude was unfounded. God's kindness was meant to lead the Jew to true repentance, not to presumption (4). Many of the things the Jews judged in the Gentiles they themselves were guilty of (1-3); and the privileges they enjoyed, through the knowledge of God's Law in particular, made their responsibility all the greater — especially at the judgment (9).

● **It's fair to everyone** (6-11). Verse 7 can be translated as follows: "Those who with patient endurance look beyond their own well-doing to the glory, honor, and incorruption God alone can give" (Barratt). The implication is that the trust of such people — whether Jews or Gentiles — is not in their good works but in God. According to the light they have, they seek God; their good works are the consequence (cf. Acts 10:2-3, 34-35). God knows the secrets of men's hearts, and according to these secrets he will judge.

Prayer

Lord, let me not evaluate myself by comparison with other people, but by comparison with Your holy commandments.

Keynote

Shall not the judge of all the earth do right?

Two Laws

● **The law of nature** (14). This is the name given to that *sense of moral responsibility* which separates man from even the highest animals. Every time we say, "I ought," we imply that there is Someone who expects us to do the right rather than the wrong thing; and that we are capable of knowing which is which; and that we are accountable to him for our decision.

It is called "the law of nature" because people arrive at it instinctively, by the light of nature. There is something deep within every man which seems to tell him, for example, that it is better to be brave than cowardly, generous than selfish, kind than cruel.

● **The law of God** (17). Up till now the Gentiles had been groping their way, as it were, with a compass (the law of nature) while the Jews had been supplied with a large scale and accurate map (the law of God).

But despite their great advantage, the Jews had blundered again and again, and also blamed the Gentiles (who had much more of an excuse than they) for committing the same offences. Could we possibly have a greater example of hypocrisy? No wonder Paul reproved them so sharply in this chapter!

Prayer

Save me, O Lord, from the sin of hypocrisy: from condemning others for the things I do myself.

Keynote

"You who say...do you?"

Inward or Outward?

● **Genuine life?** Paul brings his argument to a logical conclusion here. He tells his Jewish readers, in effect, that it is the life of a man which counts, and that *circumcision* (the old covenant sign) and the *Law* are of no personal value whatever, unless they make you a better person. In other words (reverting to yesterday's comparison), the Gentile who obeys his compass is better off, and more pleasing to God, than the Jew who disobeys his map. Applying all this to ourselves, we can say that "he is a Christian which is one inwardly" (29).

● **Or empty show?** I may be baptized, be an active church member, and possess a beautiful Bible; but unless there is something solid behind those outward symbols of Christian profession, I am like the fig tree in the parable; a mass of leaves, perhaps, but without any fruit (Luke 13:6-9).

Thought: We might say that chapter 1 applies today to those who come from pagan homes, where God is never mentioned, and where church on Sunday is unheard of. If that is so, then chapter 2 applies to those who have all the benefits of a Christian home. How carefully this second group must guard against the sins of fault-finding (1), hypocrisy (22) and formalism (29)!

Prayer

Grant, O Lord, that my outward profession of faith may be matched by an inner holiness of life.

Keynote

"Inwardly"

Four Objections

Paul answers four objections:

a) "What advantage is there then in being a Jew and in having these privileges" (1)? "Chiefly the fact that the Jewish people were entrusted with the Word of God for the whole world" (2).

b) "But doesn't the fact that so many Jews have disbelieved God cancel God's side of the agreement" (3)? "Not at all; for the faithlessness of one party to the agreement does not impair God's trustworthiness" (4).

c) "But if our sin shows up God's righteousness in a stronger light, isn't he unjust in condemning us for it" (5)? "No; if he were to condone sin at all, how could he judge the world" (6)?

d) "But if the outcome of our sin in some way increases the glory of God, why should we not continue in sin" (7)? "Such a charge has actually been levelled against some of us, but those who make it stand self-condemned" (8). Why? Paul (see 6:2) shows that the true Christian regards himself as "dead to sin."

Question: If the Jews were held *responsible* because they possessed the Old Testament, how much more responsible does God hold us who have both the Old and the New Testaments?

Prayer

O Lord, give me a hatred of sin, that I may never want to continue in it.

Keynote

"Let God be true"

Man's Condition

● **All are guilty.** In the first two chapters, Paul has accused first the Gentiles and then the Jews. Now he pronounces sentence upon them both. All are "under sin" (9) and therefore all are "guilty before God" (19).

In 1967 an oil tanker was wrecked off the English coast. Millions waited anxiously to see how far along the beaches her polluting oil would spread, threatening marine life and ports, business and vacation prospects. This compares with the awful polluting progress of sin into human nature, of which we read here. It begins with the *mind,* or heart (11,12); from there it makes its way into our *speech* (13,14; cf. James 3); and finally, it infects our *actions* (15,16).

● **The Law can't save us.** Is there any detergent that will cleanse this poisonous stream? The Law diagnoses man's problem, but it is helpless to do anything about it. No one can justify himself before God by a perfect performance of what the Law demands; in fact, "it is the straightedge of the Law that shows us how crooked we are" (20, Phillips).

● **Man's unchanging condition** (10-18) simply underlines his need of the unchanging Savior, and the way is now open for Paul to declare God's way of putting men right with himself.

Question: If the Law can't save us, what can?

Prayer

O Lord, cleanse me from my sin, and renew a right spirit within me.

Keynote

"White as snow"

Hope for All!

**VERSE
: THE WEEK
Romans 5:1**

"Is there any hope?" we might ask if we had to end at verse 20. "Yes," Paul declares. "God himself has taken the initiative and provided a way of putting men right with himself" (21-26).

● **God's part: justification** (24,26). God reckons to a sinner, through faith (25,27), the righteousness of Christ, declaring the sinner just and right before him. The cost was the death of his Son as the propitiation for our sins (25).

God's reaction to sin is wrath and displeasure. Christ by his death on the cross for our sins, propitiated the wrath of God and rendered God well disposed to his people. God has thus shown himself righteous in the just punishment of sin at the cross, and so he is rightly able to justify all who believe in his Son.

● **Man's part: faith** (25). Nine times the words "faith" and "believe" occur here. While forgiveness, made possible by Christ's death, is available to all, it is only enjoyed by those who put their trust in Christ as their own Savior.

The word "faith" is used in contrast to "works" (27,28). This means that we are made right with God not by good deeds, but by faith in what Christ has done, and "remission (forgiveness) of sins" (25) is not a reward or a wage, but a gift which can be received only by faith

Prayer

Fill me, Lord, with wonder and gratitude for "the love that drew salvation's plan and the grace that brought it down to man."

Keynote

"By faith"

Righteousness Cannot Be Earned

Paul now sets out to show that "justification by faith alone" is not a new idea which he thought up, but that it is found in God's dealing with man from the first. No two men were more respected in Jewish history than Abraham and David, and they were both put right with God, or justified, not because they deserved to be, but through faith in what God had done for them. Faith, therefore, was accepted, so to speak, in the place of the righteousness which they could not produce.

This is a most important point, for we still find two attitudes to God in the world.

● **"Of debt"** (4). There are those who feel that a decent life, kindness to others, regular worship, will earn God's favor and forgiveness. He will be obliged to reward us, they think, much as an employer is obliged to pay for work done — not granting a favor, but giving a due.

● **"Of grace"** (4). But the Bible takes quite the opposite view. Our good deeds are just not good enough to earn God's favor, and even the best of them are stained with pride. Our only hope is to receive the pardon which God offers us not as a debt, but as a gift, not because of what we are, but because of what he has done.

Prayer

Lord, I am glad that forgiveness does not depend on what I can do, but on my trust in what You have already done for me.

Keynote

Not a debt, but a favor

Faith, Not Rites

The questions which Paul asks in these chapters are those of a real or perhaps imaginary objector; and his references to Abraham and David invite the question in verse 9: **"Does this prove that God's favor is bestowed only on the Jews, or on all mankind?"** (NEB).

It was quite a fair question, and Paul answers it by showing that Abraham was justified by faith some time before he received the outward sign of circumcision which marked the special relationship of the Jews to God. The order in his experience was first *faith,* then *justification,* and finally the sign of *circumcision.*

By reversing this order, the Jews substitute a formal, dead religion for a spiritual one. They also excluded the Gentiles from God's favor by making circumcision and not faith the necessary qualification. The epistle to the Galatians was written to refute this grave error, and even today we have echoes of it in those who insist that it is some outward rite which makes a man a Christian rather than faith in Jesus Christ. Circumcision then, and baptism today, are of little use — and can even be misleading — unless accompanied by faith.

Prayer

Lord, I am grateful that the Gospel is not confined to any race or class, but that it can reach even me.

Keynote

"Walk in the steps of that faith"

Faith

● **The priority of faith.** Not only did faith come before circumcision, it also came before the Law. This underlines the two points that Paul has been making: first, that Abraham himself was justified by faith and not by obedience to a moral code; and second, that God's favor was not just for Abraham but for all mankind, whether Jew or Gentile (23-25).

● **The power of faith.** Verses 18-21 are in parenthesis. They deal with the quality of Abraham's faith. It is as though Paul said, "While we are on the subject of Abraham's faith, just consider for a moment how strong it was." What Abraham was asked to believe must have seemed impossible and fantastic. If he had paused to consider the problem, he might well have "staggered" (20; the word is also translated "waver" in James 1:6). But we read that "he considered not"!

● **What is faith?** It is trust in the character and ability of someone else. Sometimes unreliable people break promises they have the power to keep; and sometimes weak people make promises they have no power to keep. God is different. He is absolutely reliable and infinitely strong. We may have complete trust in both his character and his ability.

Prayer

O Lord, I thank You that in Your goodness and power I may have complete confidence.

Keynote

"Fully persuaded"

Justification

In this chapter Paul develops the great theme of justification by faith.

● **The meaning of justification.** It means to be "reckoned right" in God's sight. It does not just mean to be "let off," but rather to be legally acquitted, as though I had done nothing wrong at all.

● **The method of justification.** It springs in the first place from God's great "love" (8) toward us in refusing to let us perish. It was made possible by the "blood" (9) of Christ; that is, by his death in our place on the cross. We receive this justification by "faith" (1) in Jesus Christ.

● **The results of justification.** It means, of course, that we are "reconciled to God" (10). Although the quarrel between us was entirely our fault, he has taken the initiative and restored the broken friendship. This means that there is now *"peace"* between us (1), and freedom to enjoy his presence. It means that there is *"hope"* (4-5); that is, a confident assurance of salvation (9), and that God has prepared a place for us in heaven. It means also that there is *"joy"* (11) and that thoughts of God fill us with happiness, whereas once they filled us with gloom.

Prayer

Help me, O Lord, to know that I am justified because of the difference it makes in my daily life.

Keynote

"Peace with God"

Two Men and the Grace of God

"In God's sight," said Thomas Goodwin, "there are two men — Adam and Jesus Christ — and these two have all other men hanging at their girdle strings." This expressive picture fairly sums up much of what Paul seeks to convey.

● **Adam.** He sets before us the devastating consequences of Adam's sin: sin entered the world through Adam's sin, and through sin death; death has spread throughout the whole human race because everyone has sinned (12).

● **Christ.** But thank God, through our Lord Jesus Christ a new factor has entered into things — the grace of God (15). God has made possible to us a righteousness, and this righteousness breaks into, and lifts us out of, the inevitable cycle of sin and death, and brings us into the happy cycle of righteousness and life (21).

In presenting Christ to us as the "last Adam," Paul underlines the perfection of all that he has done for us, both by his obedient life and his sacrificial death. Where Adam failed, Christ succeeded. He showed himself competent to undo the devastating consequences of Adam's sin. Adam's sin brought upon us guilt; Christ's obedience brings to us righteousness. Thus instead of death reigning in our lives leading to death, grace reigns through righteousness leading to life (21).

Prayer

O Lord, thank You that "where sin increased, grace abounded all the more."

Keynote

What shall we say then? (6:1)

Dead and Alive

To help us understand this chapter, let us imagine an Englishman who becomes a naturalized American. If this "conversion" is going to be a success, then he must consider himself to be "dead" as an Englishman and "alive" as an American. England has no more claim upon him, and he owes that country no loyalty. Gradually, no doubt, the customs, tastes, standards and habits of an Englishman will begin to fall from him, and perhaps even his British accent will fall away. He is "dead to England," and will not want to "still live in it" (2).

On the other hand, as an American he will begin to "walk in newness of life" (4). It is America now, and no longer England, which has his allegiance and affection; and it is American standards which he will accept, and American habits and customs which he will try to cultivate.

The significance of baptism is recalled (3-4) because it expresses our determination, in the light of our wonderful union with Christ, to live a new life through the power of God's enabling Spirit—the same Spirit who raised our Savior from the dead (4; cf. Romans 1:4; Ephesians 1:19-20).

Prayer

O Lord, help me to become in practice what You have declared me to be in principle.

Keynote

"Newness of life"

"Reckon Yourselves"

VERSE OF THE WEEK
Romans 6:23

● **"Dead to sin."** Because Jesus Christ died on the cross, it is as though each one of us had died for his or her own sin. Sin is pictured as a slave-master from whom we have been released by death (7), and to whom, therefore, no further allegiance is due or service expected.

● **"Alive to God."** In the same way, when Christ rose from the dead we were identified with his resurrection, and it is as though each of us had individually risen from the grave to "live with him" (8) "unto God" (11).

● **"So reckon yourselves."** And so in verse 11 Paul tells us to do the sensible thing and by faith to "reckon" ourselves "to be dead indeed unto sin, but alive unto God." The word "reckon" is interesting. It is used in Mark 15:28 where Jesus "was *numbered* with the transgressors." (He was not a transgressor, but he was "reckoned" as one.) It is used in Romans 4:5 where Abraham's faith was *"counted* for righteousness." (It was not righteousness, but in God's eyes it "counted" as such.) In the same way we were not, of course, literally crucified or raised from the dead, but we are to count it as though we have been, and live our lives accordingly.

Prayer

Lord, I am grateful that because Jesus died and rose again it counts as though I had done the same, and that therefore all my sins may be forgiven, and I may be accounted righteous.

Keynote

"Reckon" by faith

Yield

Today we find another practical secret of successful Christian living. It is in verse 13.

"Yield ..." The word is sometimes translated "present," and suggests a soldier presenting arms in respect and loyalty to a king. **"...your members..."** The word means "bodily organs," for the Lord wants to possess every part of us for use in his service. "Mine are the *hands* to do thy work, my *feet* shall run for thee, my *lips* shall sound the glorious news. Lord, here am I, send me."

"...as instruments..." Think of the skilled surgeon or dentist and the marvels he can work with instruments which are completely in his control. So the Lord wants our minds, hands, feet and lips to be instruments he can use.

"...of righteousness..." There may have been a time when our "members" were used for selfish and even wicked purposes. Think how Saul of Tarsus misused his powers before they were dedicated to Christ, and then think of the good they were used to do.

"...unto God." It is the God who has loved us and done so much for us who invites us to put ourselves and all that we have at his disposal. Dare we refuse?

Prayer

Lord, take every power I possess and use them to bring others to know Christ as their Savior.

Keynote

I yield, God wields.

Rewards

● **The fruit of sin** (21). You might think that a life free from the control of righteousness and wholly dedicated to sin (20) would produce some lasting results: excitement, pleasure, experience, perhaps. But "what was the gain? Nothing but what now makes you ashamed" (21, NEB). From the very earliest times (see Genesis 3) shame has been the first fruits of sin. The things which make us blush to remember are not our disappointments, our illnesses, our failures, or even our ignorance; they are our sins. In vain we look for their fruit, but there is none; "the worm, the canker and the grief are mine alone."

● **"The wages of sin"** (23). "The servants of sin" (20) receive their wages all right, but what a terrible thing it is! "For the wages of sin *is death.*" In other words, the penalty for choosing to live without God in this life is to be compelled to live without him in the world to come; for "death" means banishment from his presence forever.

● **The result of sanctification.** To those who "become servants to God" (22), their fruit is a holy life, with all the marvelous influence it can exert; and their reward (not "wages" but a "gift") is "eternal life through Jesus Christ our Lord" (23).

Prayer

O Lord, help me always to remember the bitter, inescapable consequences of sin.

Keynote

Wages or gift?

Two Marriages

"**Called to freedom**" is a fair description of the Christian's vocation. Paul has already illustrated freedom from sin in terms of the relationship between a slave and a master (6:15-23), now he illustrates freedom from law in terms of the relationship between a wife and her husband. The key thought is that death breaks the bond between husband and wife.

● **Marriage to the Law.** Before our conversion we were "married" or "yoked" to the Law, and the fruit of our union was sin leading to death. Far from enabling us to acquire merit before God, the Law served to show us only how sinful we are. Marriage to the Law could result only in sin and death.

● **Our union with Christ.** Through the death of Christ we have died to the Law, and are married now to Christ. Our spiritual union with Christ — a relationship far deeper and stronger than human marriage because it is eternal — makes us productive for God (4). We find the service of Christ perfect freedom: the indwelling Holy Spirit provides us with the desire and the dynamic to serve God and to live for him (6).

The death of Christ becomes more and more wonderful as we ponder it (4). The more we understand Christ's sacrificial death, the more urgent becomes the appeal for holy living.

Prayer

"*I cannot work my soul to save, for that my Lord hath done; but I would work like any slave for love of God's dear Son.*"

Keynote

"**Married to another**"

The Place of the Law

Today Paul hastens to correct any possible impression his readers may have gotten that there is anything wrong with the Law itself. Certainly not! It was "holy, and just, and good" (12). The Law, however, did three things with regard to sin.

a) It defined sin (7). It drew the frontiers between good and evil in clear and unmistakable ways, so that wrong could be recognized.

b) It revived sin (9). Sometimes people say to us about a certain practice, "You know it is against the law, don't you?" And for the first time we realize that something we had been doing for ages is actually a punishable offense. That is what Paul meant in verse 9. God's Law "revived" sin by showing us that to practice it makes us guilty in his eyes, and therefore that we "do worthily deserve to be punished."

c) It punished sin (10-13). This follows quite logically from the previous point. Once something becomes an offense, it must be punished, and, as we have seen, "the wages of sin is death." Sin has always been wrong, ever since time began; but only when the Law came could the sinner be called a "transgressor," and therefore guilty as well as unclean.

Prayer

Lord, I thank You for the Law, and that it defines so clearly for us the deadly nature of sin.

Keynote

"In the absence of Law, sin is a dead thing" (8, NEB)

The Christian Conflict

The key to understanding this vital passage is realizing that Paul writes it as a Christian believer. Whereas in verses 7-13 he uses the past tense — describing his pre-Christian days — in these verses he uses the present tense.

● **There is a battle in the Christian life.** It is against the world, the flesh and the devil. Here Paul deals primarily with *the flesh*. The power of indwelling sin is so strong that we find ourselves not doing what we really want to do, but doing what we really loathe (15). The conflict is agonizing and wretched. With our mind we serve the Law of God, but with our flesh we serve the law, or principle, of sin (25). *How can our mind gain control over our flesh?* Thank God, through our Lord Jesus Christ, there is an answer, by the power of his Holy Spirit — and chapter 8 sees the unfolding of this glorious principle.

● **We should not minimize the battle.** Whatever Paul says later about God's provision, it does not take away the principle of conflict. We do not lose our sinful flesh in this earthly life.

Our awareness of inner corruption increases as we grow in the knowledge of God. If a soldier is at war, he is not to blame if he has to fight; he is to blame if he does not use the resources available to him.

Prayer

Lord, help me always to enjoy the victory made possible by the indwelling presence and power of the Holy Spirit.

Keynote

I ought, I want, I can't; but HE CAN!

Our Resources

● **"In Christ!"** "There is therefore now no condemnation for those who are *in Christ Jesus"* (1). That is where the Christian *stands.*

The word translated "condemnation" probably means "the condemnation following sentence" — what we would call "penal servitude." Having been justified, Paul reasons, there is no reason why we should go on paying the penalty for our sin as if we had never been pardoned and freed by Christ. Tragically that happens when we take our eyes off the finished work of Christ, and lose our appreciation of our position "in him." God intends that we should rejoice in the justification which he has so wonderfully provided for us.

● **"After the Spirit"** (1,4,5). God has made a wonderful provision, through the Holy Spirit's indwelling, for us to obey and please him (4,8). Before new birth the ruling principle in any life is that of sin leading to death. When we are born from above a new principle enters our lives — the law of the Spirit of life (2). He can enable us effectively to overcome the principle of sin in our flesh and to fulfill God's law. The conflict will not cease during this present life; but all the time we allow the Spirit to control us — by obedience — our old nature is compelled to give way.

Prayer

Lord, may the Holy Spirit govern my thinking, my desiring, and my willing.

Keynote

"Spiritually minded"

The True Christian

**VERSE
OF THE WEEK
Romans 8:9**

How would you define a *true Christian?* There are, no doubt, many answers to that question, but the one given us here is that he is *a person whose life is controlled by the Holy Spirit.* The Holy Spirit has come to "dwell" within him (9-10), and he is "led by the Spirit" (14) in his daily life and conduct. There is then evidence within and without that we belong to God. Now, notice the work of the Spirit in the heart of the Christian. What does he do there?

● **"Spirit of life"** (2). First, he will "bring to our whole being new strength and vitality" (11, Phillips). Through his power we shall be able to live a life which is pleasing to God and "mortify the deeds of the body" (13). This means that our actions will no longer be dictated simply by the desires of our senses, but by the will of God.

● **"Spirit of adoption"** (15). Second, the Holy Spirit will bring to our hearts the assurance that we are the children of God. Every Christian has this sense that he is related to God in a special personal way. It is not easy to explain it logically. It is a kind of instinct created by the Holy Spirit. Prayer becomes natural to him. Not only can we say "Great God..." but "Abba (literally "Daddy"), Father."

Prayer

Father, may Your Holy Spirit fill my life, and control my every thought and word and action.

Keynote

"Indwelt"

Suffering and Glory

Suffering and glory (18) went together in our Lord's experience (Matthew 16:21; Luke 24:26) and are found in ours (17). Suffering (see verses 35-36) is a feature of this present time. But after suffering comes glory, which believers enter in the life to come, through being brought into the likeness of Christ. Glory is not only a compensation for suffering, but it actually grows out of it (cf. 2 Corinthians 4:16-18).

● **The Spirit gives us hope** (19-25). Christian "hope" is not a vaguely optimistic attitude toward the future, but rather a confident expectation of receiving something which has been promised. For what then do we hope?

(a) *For a full revelation of the glory of God* (18),

(b) *For the release of the whole universe* (20-22) from bondage,

(c) *For the completion of our own personal redemption* through Christ (23-24).

● **The Spirit gives us help.** The Holy Spirit helps us by maintaining the hope within us while we wait for the redemption of our bodies, and by coming to our aid in the face of every weakness. He intercedes for us (26), not on his own account but on Christ's. He does not plead for us, as does Christ, but he puts pleas into our mouths or lays burdens of prayer upon our hearts.

Prayer

Lord, burden my heart with those things You want me to pray for.

Keynote

No suffering, no glory

"All Things"

Three times in this passage the phrase "All...things" occurs (28,32,37). It aptly describes God's abundant grace toward the Christian.

Verse 28. Sometimes it is difficult to see just what part sorrow, disappointment or failure can have in God's purpose for a Christian's life, but we must believe that he can use these things, as well as everything else, for our ultimate good.

Verse 32. If God has given us his most valuable treasure, in the Person of his Son, will he withhold from us the other things that we need for living our Christian lives? Whatever our needs may be (for wisdom, perhaps, or patience, or courage) he is able to supply them from his own inexhaustible riches.

Verse 37. What does it mean to be "more than conquerors"? Both Phillips and the NEB speak of enjoying "overwhelming victory." In other words, the Christian does not just scrape home by the skin of his teeth, but he "spoils" his defeated attackers, and is made rich by his conquest. He does not just survive the threats of verse 35, but surmounts them; and because of them is a stronger, more positive and wealthier Christian altogether.

Prayer

Lord, I am grateful for the wonderfully complete way in which You control and cover the lives of all who trust in You.

Keynote

"All things"

Your Introduction to Psalms 22, 23, and 30

Psalm 22 is one of the most remarkable Psalms in the entire Psalter. It traces the experience of one who is suffering intensely from a long-term illness. Because of its length and intensity, his friends mock him and he feels forsaken by God himself (22:1). Jesus knew Psalm 22 by heart. On the cross, he so identified with the author, that he cried out its opening words, "My God, my God, why hast thou forsaken me?" The Psalm has always been seen by the church as a foreshadowing of Jesus' death by crucifixion. Indeed, the parallels between it and the Gospel accounts are remarkable evidence of the inspiration of both by the same Holy Spirit.

Psalm 23 is the best known and most beloved Psalm. God is pictured as a shepherd, guiding and protecting the Psalmist, his sheep. He guides him through difficulties and provides for him abundantly, ultimately bringing him home to himself. Can anyone read this Psalm and not feel sure it was written by the lonely shepherd boy who later became David, the king?

We do not know how, but the writer of Psalm 30 has stared death in the face: "Thou hast brought me up from Sheol." He prospered and felt himself secure, but God allowed tragedy to enter his life (30:7). In answer to his cry, God rescued him, giving him gladness in the place of suffering.

As you prayerfully meditate upon them, these and other Psalms will provide you with renewed faith, divine comfort, and hope in the midst of trouble.

The Great Test

Today, as in the Psalmist's day, many people turn up their noses at our faith. "You're kidding yourself," they say. "It's self-deception. You imagine all kinds of 'answers to prayer' in what are really coincidences. You have feelings you think come from God, but really they are auto-suggestion!"

Usually it's easy to answer this kind of criticism, or else just ignore it. *But not when our world falls apart.* That's when all the cynical remarks come back, and suddenly become a real challenge to our faith. So it was with David.

● **The force of suffering.** Look at one or two verses. It's *real* suffering — meaningless (1), crushing (6), terrifying (12-13), draining (15), humiliating (18). Worst of all, days and nights go by, and God (if there *is* a God) does nothing (2).

● **The power of faith.** How to come through? Learn from David. Faith must feed on God's Word (3-4), or starve to death. Faith must draw from its own past experiences (9-10). Above all, faith must fasten its eyes on the Lord, even in times of doubt (1), and *keep them there,* until the answer comes (19-21)!

Think ● How much of this psalm was true of Jesus, in his suffering and death?

Pray

for all who are suffering and have no one else to pray for them.

Keynote

When you hit bottom, Christ is there

When You Come Though

Look what can happen when one person gets an experience of God's power that is real!

● **An experience shared between you and the Lord.** In the case of David, it's in verse 24. God did something for him, heard his prayer, set him right. That is where it has to start.

● **An experience shared between you and the believers.** There has to be a group you can talk to, that speaks your language, that will praise God with you (22). If you don't have a group like that, find one. You need it; they need you.

● **An experience shared between you and the world.** That group shouldn't be an "in-group" — exclusive and self-centered. It must exist for the world (27-28). The group comes alive as the members share their experiences of Jesus Christ; then the message spreads across the city and across the country and across the world. *This is most important;* otherwise you have a "clique," and that is no use to anyone.

If enough Christians get turned on like this, we can change our world (29). It may take a generation (30-31), but we can do it.

Think ● Are you making as much noise about Jesus Christ as others are about war or poverty or race?

Pray

that a mighty movement for Christ may sweep through our world.

Keynote

"The ends of the earth" (27)

The Best Therapy

Everyone is seeking therapy; here's a therapeutic Psalm with something for most.

● **Do you feel disoriented?** The sickness most of us battle against is not physical but psychological. The world has become too big and complicated; it moves too fast; we can't keep up. So we live with tension, we're driven by pressures, we've lost our bearings. Verses 1-3 are God's remedy. Here's a bigger entity even than the universe — the Lord himself. Here's something real to lock on to, to stay on track.

● **Do you feel dismayed?** The "valley of the shadow of death" is every situation that involves you in insecurity, danger and fear. You may be in it today. Then read verse 4.

● **Do you feel discarded?** A number? Unwanted? Like the "end of line" that gets sold off cheap? Then look at verses 5 and 6. You are in for a royal feast! Jesus Christ is the host; you are the number-one guest! In his eyes, you're special. Right now — and forever.

Think ● **To tackle *circumstances* is like tackling *symptoms*. Tackle *yourself* and you get to the root of the matter.**

Pray

for a controlled personality, held together by the Lord himself!

Keynote

With Christ you can survive

Mourning into Dancing

This Psalm has a special message for those who feel that God has let them down. It was written after a terrible experience of severe distress — possibly an illness that was nearly fatal (see verse 3).

● **God's goodness** (1-5). It begins with praise for God's help and healing. The Psalmist sees his distressing experience as a temporary thing, turned by God's kindness into blessing and joy. "Weeping" — he thinks of it as a person visiting his house — only stays overnight. "Joy" comes to stay permanently (5).

● **His recent trouble** (6-10). The Psalmist recalls how he had seemed immune to trouble (6), but suddenly it descended on him as though God had turned his face away from him (7). He cried to God in agony, admitting his own utter helplessness in the face of death (9-10). Contrast this with his earlier confidence (7a).

● **His new resolve** (11-12). Now he has a new resolve. His mourning has been turned into dancing for joy (11). His sad clothes have given way to happier dress. But he sees that all this has a purpose — that his whole being ("soul" here means "life") should express praise and thanksgiving to the God who had delivered him (12).

Pray

that when things seem black, the Lord will help you to trust him.

Keynote

"That my soul may praise thee and not be silent"

Your Introduction to 1 John

Even though this letter does not name its author, John the Evangelist has been so identified from earliest times. Its style and doctrine are so similar to the Gospel of John, that 1 John must have been written by the same author, probably toward the end of the first century.

While this letter conveys apostolic doctrine, it also clearly reflects John's personal experience of God. He makes it clear at the outset that what he teaches is not based on hearsay, but on actual contact with Jesus Christ. And he contends that such contact is essential for a proper relationship both to God and between one another (1:1-4).

The balance of this letter, written to Christians in general, may be outlined as follows:

I. Walk in the light (1:5-2:29)
   A. By breaking with sin (1:8-2:2)
   B. By keeping the commandments, especially the law of love (2:3-11)
   C. By detachment from the world (2:12-17)
   D. By guarding against Christ's enemies (2:18-29)

II. Live as God's children (3:1-4:6)
   A. By breaking with sin (3:3-9)
   B. By keeping the commandments, especially the law of love (3:10-24)
   C. By guarding against Christ's enemies and against the world (4:1-6)

III. Love and faith (4:7-5:13)
   A. Love (4:7-5:4)
   B. Faith (5:5-12)
   C. Conclusion (5:13)

IV. Postscript (5:14-21)
   A. Prayer for sinners (5:14-17)
   B. Summary of letter (5:18-21)

John was a gentle, practical man, and you will find his book full of Christian teaching.

Spirited Living in a Dark World

VERSE OF THE WEEK
I John 1:7

John wrote in days startlingly like our own. Change was in the air; the structures of society were crumbling; old values were no longer accepted. Permissive morals were running riot; strange new cults went in and out of fashion every year. It was hard for Christians to hold steady. Perhaps this letter was a "circular" to churches in John's area.

He is never pessimistic. He doesn't live in the past. He knows the *present* need. He's utterly positive about *Christ,* and about *faith,* and about *right living.* Just as we should be.

Today's reading is an example. In contrast to the confusion all around, John proclaims two things that Christ offers:

● **Reality** (1-4). Christian faith rests on solid facts. Again and again John claims to have been in personal contact with Christ: he mentions three of his five senses (which?). How can you deny evidence like that?

● **Renewal** (5-10). To have one's conscience washed clean is no illusion, nor is it irrelevant in a largely neurotic society. Read again the conditions for this inner cleansing.

● **In what forms are people most conscious of "sin" nowadays?**

Pray *that you may always be honest with God about your life.*

Dawn Is Breaking!

I'm sure you have a picture of what John is saying here. He sees darkness dragging on like a night that never seems to end. But at last there is a lightening in the east, and the first rays of the sun feel their way up into the dark sky. The shadows begin to melt away, and fear gives way to peace.

"The darkness is passing away and the true light is already shining" (8). How wonderful to think that since the coming of Christ the darkness in this world can never be absolute again; there is always light, light which can never be put out! And what is the light?

● **The light is Christ himself.** By removing the pollution of sin (1-2), Christ shines into darkened lives. He gives sight to the eyes and gladness to the heart. More than this, he is the Example of how one's life can be full of light, even when there is still much darkness around (6).

● **The light is every Christian.** If Christ is the Sun, each Christian is a ray, communicating the Light further and further into the darkness (8-10). What is the main way he does this (10)?

● **Why do you think there is still so much darkness in the world? Is the true light shining clearly today? What part do you have in this?**

Pray

for the places in the world which seem to you to be darkest.

Warnings

● **A triple message.** John's message is to all whose sins are forgiven and in whom the Word of God abides. The three groups he distinguishes (children, fathers and young men) represent the whole spectrum of the church, at every stage of spiritual experience.

● **A triple warning.** He follows with a solemn warning against a trinity of evil:

The lust of the flesh, which represents any giving in to our lower natures; *the lust of the eyes,* which applies to being fascinated by the glamour and superficial attraction of evil; *the pride of life,* which says, "We've got it all figured out, and can do it by ourselves."

● **All are symptoms of "worldliness" — that is, loving "the world" (15) rather than the Father.** *"The world," in context here, is simply human society organized as though God did not exist.* Christians are to be careful that they do not align themselves with it, even unconsciously.

● **Our weapons against the world,** and against "antichrists" (misleading imitators and opponents of Christ) are the anointing of the Holy Spirit (20) and the simple, original Gospel (24) — both are available to us all.

● **"All that is in the world...is not of the Father" (16). But if God created everything, what can this verse mean?**

Pray

that you may be strong to overcome evil in yourself and the world.

Purity Is Not a Joke

I imagine you have come across the idea that "purity" is a quaint, old-fashioned concept. Perhaps someone has made fun of *you* because you stick to standards of "purity." Well, take encouragement from John's words: "Everyone who has this hope in Christ keeps himself pure, just as Christ is pure" (3, TEV). But *why* should I keep myself pure?

● **Because I am God's child.** This thought runs through all these verses. God has told me what kind of living pleases him, and that's the life I want to live.

● **Because I am Christ's follower.** In Christ I see human character at its highest. One day I'll be like him (2). Why not start now (3)?

● **Because I am the Spirit's temple.** I have "God's nature"; I am "born of God" (9). So God's Spirit changes my desire and I become like my new Father!

Verse 9 doesn't mean that a Christian is *incapable* of committing a single sin. It means *he cannot possibly go on living an impure life.* If he belongs to God's "family," the "family likeness" is bound to show up.

● **What would you say to a Christian who was worried because his life didn't seem to be good enough to please God?**

that "the works of the devil" may be destroyed in YOU.

Loving and Hating

John shows us two ways of life and where each one leads to. Each of us chooses one or the other.

● **The way of love.** *It begins* in verse 11: "We should love one another." *It continues* in action in verse 18 (TEV): "True love, which shows itself in action." And *it leads* to verse 16: "We...ought to give our lives for our brothers." Now, obviously we're not *all* called upon to sacrifice our lives, but Jesus spoke of giving a cup of cold water to a thirsty man, or visiting a sick friend, or giving your coat to a needy person. Christ sees no difference between these acts — *only whether or not you do what the love of Christ demands in the situation.*

● **The way of hate.** *It begins* in verse 14: "He who fails to love." *It continues* in verse 15: "He who hates his brother" — that's one stage worse. And *it leads* to verse 12: "He murdered his brother." Not everyone who's lacking in love ends up as a murderer, but the Bible doesn't see too much difference (15). *It's as serious to leave someone without help as it is to do him actual harm.*

● **I may murder someone, or I may just "close my heart against him" (17). In what ways are these actions the same, and in what ways are they different?**

Pray that love may dominate all your actions, whether great or small.

Such a Simple Secret

Would you believe it? Within days we could transform our sick society into heaven on earth! No doubt about it! It could happen just like *that!*

● **Such a simple secret!** It comes 27 times in these verses. It's "love." Although this may seem obvious, even trite in our decade, be assured that John is writing with deep feeling. Every situation could be radically changed if every person would act in a loving way.

● **What a difference it would make!** Just imagine. *Love* in the home, *love on the farm, love* on the roads, *love* between employer and employee, *love* between nations, *love* between social classes, *love* between races — not just talk, but the real thing.

● **And what's to prevent it?** It's God's will for his children, as this passage teaches us. And he has made it possible for us to love as he himself has loved. Through Christ we may share his own Spirit!

● **Yet men refuse!** And the world struggles on from one crisis to the next; men refuse to turn from sin, and have to be satisfied with second-class happiness.

● **Why don't some people let love rule their actions? Are you for your part living the life of love to the full?**

Pray that in this hate-torn world many may see Christ's love in his people, and be drawn to him.

"We Shall Overcome!"

Christians are overcomers! We overcome "the world," which means everything the devil brings against us — temptations of all kinds, opposition, confusion, and so on. And the *means* by which we overcome is — "our faith" (4).

But "our faith" has three parts: *belief* (1), *love* (2) and *obedience* (3). Look at it this way:

- **We "overcome" the world's confused beliefs.** Man's beliefs have never been more confused. There is every variation of Christianity, plus astrology, witchcraft, Eastern mysticism, atheism, and everything in between. Against this confusion, we hold fast to Jesus as Christ and Son of God (1,5).

- **We "overcome" the world's twisted emotions.** Emotionally many people are tearing themselves apart in this complex, technological age. For the Christian, the one overriding emotion is *love*. Everything else falls into place.

- **We "overcome" the world's uncertain morals.** Young people are in a tough position today. With so many voices coming at them, how can they know what is right and what is wrong? The Christian answers: "Obey God's Word, and stick with it!"

- **How far do you consider your own life to be an "overcoming" life?**

Thank God

for the victory he has promised you through Jesus Christ.

It's Great to Be Sure!

VERSE
OF THE WEEK
1 John 3:23

Certainty is one of the great blessings God has given to us Christians. Unbelievers may say we are presumptuous and pigheaded, but we should never let this kind of talk rob us of our assurance about Jesus Christ. Note three "certainties" in today's reading.

a) We know that Jesus is the Son of God.
God himself has "borne witness" to it (9). How? In his Word, in Jesus' miracles, in raising Jesus from the dead, in changing people's lives — and in the heart of everyone who believes (10).

b) We know that we have eternal life.

How? Read verse 13. This verse can become a turning point in your life when it is fully believed. Some who may doubt for years whether they are real Christians can be assured here that if they believe in the Name of Christ, God has *guaranteed* them eternal life.

We know that our prayers are answered.
That's in verses 14-15. Strange that we should ever doubt it! But God answers prayer in different ways, and sometimes we need to be reminded that *not one genuine prayer is ever passed over.*

● **How do you explain it when an important prayer of yours *seems* to go unanswered?**

Pray *that the church may give a confident witness to Jesus Christ.*

The following daily Bible reading aids are available from Scripture Union, published quarterly:

Discovery (Basic Series. A continuation of this book, adults and high school students.)

Encounter with God (Advanced Series)

Quest (For children ages 7-10)

Keynotes (For young people ages 11-14)

Simon and Sarah (For children ages 3-6)

For further information, write to:

U.S.A.:
Scripture Union
1716 Spruce Street
Philadelphia, Pennsylvania 19103

Canada:
Scripture Union
2100 Lawrence Ave. East
Scarborough, Ontario M1R 2Z7